D1485316

Commemoration

Síreacht: Longings for Another Ireland is a series of short, topical and provocative texts on controversial issues in contemporary Ireland.

Contributors to the *Síreacht* series come from diverse backgrounds and perspectives but share a commitment to the exposition of what may often be disparaged as utopian ideas, minority perspectives on society, polity and environment, or critiques of received wisdom. Associated with the phrase *ceól sírechtach síde* found in Irish medieval poetry, *síreacht* refers to yearnings such as those evoked by the music of the *aos sí*, the supernatural people of Irish mythology. As the title for this series, we use it to signify longings for and imaginings of a better world in the spirit of the World Social Forums that 'another world is possible'. At the heart of the mythology of the *sí* is the belief that laying beneath this world is the other world. So too these texts address the urgent challenge to imagine potential new societies and relationships, but also to recognise the seeds of these other worlds in what already exists.

Other published titles in the series are

Freedom? by Two Fuse
Public Sphere by Harry Browne

The editors of the series, Órla O'Donovan, Fiona Dukelow and Rosie Meade, School of Applied Social Studies, University College Cork, welcome suggestions or proposals for consideration as future titles in the series. Please see http://sireacht.ie/ for more information.

Commemoration

HEATHER LAIRD

Series Editors:
Órla O'Donovan, Fiona Dukelow and Rosie Meade

First published in 2018 by
Cork University Press
Youngline Industrial Estate
Pouladuff Road, Togher
Cork T12 HT6V, Ireland

British Library Cataloguing in Publication Data
A CIP catalogue record for this book is available from the British
Library.

ISBN 9781782052562

Typeset by Studio 10 Design
Printed by Hussar Books in Poland

For Helen and Siobhán

CONTENTS

FIGURES

Figure 1: Constance Markievicz in uniform with gun. Source: National Library of Ireland [NPA MGU].

Figure 2: *Insurrection*: reporter in modern clothes. Source: RTÉ Archives.

Figure 3: James Connolly on the window of the Brown Thomas department store. Source: Ronan McGreevy.

Figure 4: Paul Klee, *Angelus Novus*, 1920. Source: Public Domain – Wikimedia Commons.

ACKNOWLEDGEMENTS

In 2016, the centenary of the Easter Rising, I delivered a number of talks on the topic of commemoration. I want to thank the editors of the Síreacht series – Órla O'Donovan, Fiona Dukelow and Rosie Meade – for giving me the opportunity to transform those lectures into this book. The process of aligning my ideas regarding commemoration with the aims of the Síreacht series was both fruitful and fun. Indeed, the year that I spent working on this book was a useful reminder that research, while central to the seemingly never-ending evaluation of individual academics and whole departments, should ultimately matter in its own terms and be a source of pleasure. I also want to thank everyone at Cork University Press, particularly Maria O'Donovan, for their invaluable work in preparing this book for publication. Some of my hard-working friends and colleagues in the School of English at University College, Cork helped shape this book. Lee Jenkins deserves a special mention. Her enthusiastic response to an earlier version of my first lecture on commemoration gave me confidence in my ideas at a point in time when I had begun to doubt myself. I am lucky to be part of a large and very vibrant extended family; I want to single out, in particular, Maeve Laird, Rosaleen Dolan, Marion Dolan, Shane Laird and Róisín Allott. This book is dedicated to Helen Finney and Siobhán Coffey; Helen and Siobhán, I'm sure you're relieved that after some deliberation I decided not to conclude the acknowledgements with a cheesy inspirational quotation for you both about dealing with difficult times!

Introduction

In this book, written during Ireland's decade of centenaries, I draw on the aims of the Síreacht series to reimagine commemoration. The Síreacht collection of short books, subtitled 'Longings for Another Ireland', are designed to reinvigorate the social imagination and thus encourage speculation on alternatives to current orthodoxies. My contribution to the series commences with a critique of existing commemorative practices and mainstream history writing. The principal purpose of this critique is to open up discussion on the roads untaken in history. I propose ways that we can both make these roads visible and 'remember' them. I link the untaken roads of the past to side-branching roads in the present: real possible alternatives to dominant ways of thinking and being, outlining a radical commemoration process that would connect these two sets of roads. Land and property are recurring concerns here. However, while I ground the book in concepts and practices of land and property occupancy and usage, the ideas that I explore are relevant to the broader set of struggles concerning collective welfare that impel the Síreacht series.

The book crosses time periods and, like some of the activists and agitators it mentions, roams freely over boundaries, though in this case disciplinary ones, referring to history, literature, television drama and documentary, economics, politics, law and art. Notwithstanding its temporal range and sometimes disparate subject matter, *Commemoration* is intended as a coherent whole, pivoting on a number of key concepts. These concepts are connected in that, for the most part, each provides the foundation for a subsequent one. The distinction formed between the past and history in the opening atomising of commemoration, and the accompanying claims regarding the selective nature of the latter, for example, underpin the connections that I then make between progress and mainstream history writing. This, in turn, allows me to interrogate the concept of progress, and to distinguish between a notion of societal change that looks both to the future and to the damage of the past, and a progressivism that celebrates an unrelenting movement forward despite the devastation left in its wake. The concept of counterfactualism – understood here to be that which did not happen but could have happened – is used to reveal both the potential alternatives hidden by progressivist histories, and the futures that they could have given rise to. These unrealised yet fully realisable past futures are especially numerous, I argue, during periods of potent possibility: points in time when the future seems particularly open to being shaped by those living in the present. I employ the concept of avant-garde nostalgia, a simultaneous backward/forward look, when considering how we might disentangle a yearning for a better future from progressivism. Future thinking that is not progressivist embraces change, but draws on disparaged ways of thinking and being that were and are dismissed as obstacles to progress. When devising a title for his book *Utopia* (1516), Thomas More drew on the Greek words *ou-topos*, meaning 'no place', and *eu-topos*, meaning 'a good place'. Choosing to place emphasis on the latter of these words, I propose that the simultaneous backward/forward look, sceptical of the so-called progressive ideas that simply sustain the present order of things, is the form of utopianism most likely to result in a 'good place' that is both different to, and better than, the here and now.

Commemoration
and History

In Ireland we are currently living through a decade of centenaries marking a chain of events in Irish history that commenced with the introduction of the Third Home Rule Bill in the British House of Commons in 1912 and concluded with the establishment of the Irish Free State in 1922. At the time of the writing of this book, 2017, we have only reached the decade's midpoint, but many of us feel commemoration-saturated already. The one hundredth anniversary of the 1916 rebellion against British rule was, of course, particularly salient. On Easter Monday, 24 April 1916, approximately 1,600 Irish men and women – comprised of members of the Irish Volunteers, the Irish Citizen Army and Cumann na mBan – seized a number of strategic buildings in Dublin. Outside one of these buildings, the General Post Office (GPO) in the centre of the city, Patrick Pearse read from a document that proclaimed the establishment of an Irish Republic, and of a provisional government comprised of seven men that would oversee the establishment and administration of that Republic. Supporting actions took place in the broader Dublin area and in Enniscorthy (Wexford), Bawnard near Fermoy (Cork), Athenry (Galway), and Tralee and Banna Strand (Kerry).

In 2016, in remembrance of this day and ensuing events, including the crushing of the rebellion and the execution of some of its leaders, thousands of commemorative activities took place in cities, towns and villages throughout the island of Ireland, particularly south of the border. Some of these activities were part of the official programme of commemorations, such as the principal centennial celebrations held in Dublin on Easter Sunday and Monday. Others – most notably the parade, pageant and concert organised by the Reclaim the Vision of 1916 initiative – were associated with groups who are critical of the state and those who they claim benefit most from its policies. At regional level, Ireland's many local history societies also put on events, some of which drew attention to the contribution made by those associated with the respective area to the Rising, though most were of a more general nature. For example, the conference held by the Cork Historical and Archaeological Society in July 2016 explored issues ranging from the political and cultural climate in Cork before the Rising to the circumstances of Cork Protestants in 1916. Trade unions and campaigning organisations of various kinds likewise planned and took part in activities relating to the marking of 1916, with Ireland's largest trade union, SIPTU, covering three sides of its headquarters, Liberty Hall, with images of the insurrection.[1] Nearby, the Abbey

Theatre announced a special 1916 centenary programme, 'Waking the Nation', that sparked controversy due to its almost complete omission of female playwrights.[2] Those of us who work in the third-level educational sector, particularly in history and English departments, were under considerable pressure to ensure that the institution in which we are based was initiating and participating in at least as many centenary-related events as other Irish universities, and that our departments were at least as commemoration-active as other departments in our home university. Special commemoration committees were established in universities throughout the country with the former aim in mind. As part of its special decade of centenaries series of annual publications, *History Ireland* magazine brought out a collection of essays, *1916: Dream and Death*, on the impact of the Rising. Under the title *The Workers' Republic: James Connolly and the Road to the Rising*, SIPTU made available in one volume all of the extant issues published between 29 May 1915 and 22 April 2016 of the James Connolly-edited news-sheet, *The Workers' Republic*. Publishers competed for their share of the Rising book market with both new historical accounts of this event, sometimes referred to in the blurb as definitive, and reprints of previously published studies, often marketed as foundational. Bookshops also stocked novels set against the backdrop of 1916, such as Lia Mills' *Fallen*, which was the 2016 choice for Dublin: One City One Book.[3] Rising-themed children's publications include Joe Duffy's *Children of the Rising*[4] and *The Irish Rebellion: April 1916* (The Young Indiana Jones

Chronicles, Book 8). In the latter book, Indiana Jones, as a boy, implausibly witnesses the Rising and, even more implausibly, bumps into a number of well-known Irish literary figures, including James Joyce, W.B. Yeats and Sean O'Casey. Thankfully, the Indiana Jones franchise was not the only non-Irish publishing entity to pay attention to the Rising centenary; amongst the others that did so was *Jacobin*, a notable magazine of the American left, which dedicated an entire issue, 'Between the Risings', to the 1916 insurrection and its legacies.

The vast array of Rising memorabilia available for purchase in shops or online included 1916 commemorative calendars; 1916 commemorative posters; 1916 commemorative candles; 1916 commemorative coins; 1916 commemorative medals; 1916 commemorative stamps; 1916 commemorative mugs; 1916 commemorative plates; 1916 commemorative key rings; 1916 commemorative rings; 1916 commemorative brooches; 1916 commemorative cufflinks; 1916 commemorative pens; 1916 commemorative T-shirts; twenty-four-carat gold-plated copies of the Proclamation declaring an Irish Republic; 1916 commemorative chocolate bars, each decorated with a copy of the Proclamation (not gold-plated!) and a picture of one of its signatories; and, courtesy of Arnotts department store, tricolour-bedecked 1916 commemorative fridges with '100 Years' blazoned across the front. Wealthier collectors seeking authentica had the opportunity to bid for the actual tricolour that flew from the GPO in 1916, as it and other original Rising-related items were put up for sale at public auction.

Despite our current forced familiarity in Ireland with commemoration as a practice, one of the initial goals of this book is to defamiliarise it as a concept. What exactly is a commemoration and what form does it conventionally take? How does a commemoration compare to approaches to the past more generally? A commemoration, as may seem self-evident, mostly involves a focus on an individual past event considered significant in the history of a people, nation or state. It is a marking of the event, often taking the form of a public ceremony and/ or a monument. Sometimes this is part of a collective grieving process, as is the case with commemorations of the Holocaust, the 1948 Palestinian exodus or the Irish Famine. More often, however, it is a celebration of an event deemed to have had a largely beneficial or positive impact. It generally includes an element of critical reflection. Thus, even when the tone is largely celebratory, commemoration can incorporate some level of interrogation of the event or reflection on it. It can encompass a degree of meta-critical examination focused, as the word 'meta' suggests, not on the event itself but on the way that it is dealt with. Questions may be asked, for example, about how the event is typically narrated, what version of it is most widely accepted, what or who tends to be left out in accounts of the event, whose past it is most associated with, and whose or which interests its commemoration serves.

In most analyses of commemorative practices, particularly those offered by historians, a distinction is formed between history and memory. I want to open my discussion of commemoration by forming a more fundamental distinction: a distinction between history and the past.

> The past comprises the totality of the human experience, every step taken behind every plough by every peasant who has ever lived, every credit-card bill or tax return, every human action whether inspired by heroism or spite, every meal, every act of copulation. History, by contrast, is our selective attempt to make some sense of at least one corner of that enormous past, the process by which we put some of its chaos into order and seek to understand how and why it happened the way it did.[5]

The past, therefore, is perhaps best viewed as a chaotic multiplicity made up of countless occurrences, some of which are designated events, either at the time that they take place or at a later juncture. The Irish official Decade of Centenaries website claims that the state's centenary programme will 'commemorate each step that Ireland took between 1912 and 1922'.[6] However, the past occurrences that are commemorated in Ireland and elsewhere, at least at an official level, tend to be those that have been categorised as events and assigned a key role in a history writing that, as the aforementioned passage reminds us, is always and inevitably selective. The starting point for most historians attempting to make sense of the past and 'put some of its chaos into order' is to form a distinction between the past occurrences that are central/

significant and the past occurrences that are peripheral/insignificant. Though there have been attempts to assert otherwise, this distinction has very much shaped the state's approach to the decade of centenaries. Thus, in actuality, the project of marking 'each step that Ireland took between 1912 and 1922' is equated on the official Decade of Centenaries website with a 'programme of annual commemorations with special centenary commemorative events on the anniversaries of key events'.[7] Indeed, one of the principal functions of the Advisory Group on Centenary Commemorations established by the Irish state is to ensure 'proportionality'. This 'proportionality' is achieved, we are told, through the provision of advice that directs 'the general development of the programme and the provision of official support' towards commemorations 'relating to events, issues and processes of significance'.[8] Thus, Ireland's decade of centenaries, as is the case with commemoration more generally, is the product of the same highly selective process that transforms the past into history.

It is possible, of course, to open commemoration out to other past occurrences that have not received as much attention in mainstream history writing, but this can end up being a tokenistic endeavour. For example, in 2013 a number of centenary activities took place that marked the 1913 Lockout, a labour dispute that lasted nearly five months and involved some twenty thousand workers. Such activities were an important reminder of the resistance offered by the working class and trade unionism to exploitative work practices and poor social conditions in early twentieth-century Ireland, often at great personal cost to those involved. In some instances these centenary activities also drew attention to the assault on workers' rights in present-day neoliberal Ireland. Lockout commemorative projects included *Living the Lockout* and the Tapestry Project. *Living the Lockout*, staged by the Anu Productions team, was a site-specific performance located in a building on Henrietta Street in Dublin's north inner city that offered a history of the Lockout as experienced by a number of occupants of the house. The Tapestry Project involved the creation of a forty-five-foot long work of textile art, designed by Cathy Henderson and Robert Ballagh, to provide a visual representation of the 1913 battle between labour and capital in the fight for union recognition and the right to collective bargaining. Comprised of thirty panels, it was jointly commissioned by the National College of Art and Design and SIPTU, and collectively made. Amongst the diverse range of groups that contributed to its completion were the Irish Embroidery Guild, the Irish Patchwork Society, the Irish Countrywomen's Association, theatre groups, community activists, trade unionists, schoolteachers and pupils, prisoners, and organisations associated with people with disabilities. Following its unveiling in Liberty Hall, it was exhibited in various locations throughout the state. However, notwithstanding such innovative and ambitious initiatives, the commemoration of the Lockout has been completely dwarfed by the 1916 commemoration celebrations. The differing levels of time, attention and money devoted to the centenary anniversaries of 1913 and 1916 reflect and reinforce the status that the events that took place in Ireland in those years are assigned in the national narrative.

In the early stages of the decade of centenaries a number of Ireland's most influential historians expressed concern about the tendency of commemorative practices to produce 'bad history'.[9] Commemoration, we were warned, not only encompasses the word 'memory' but is similarly susceptible to 'falsification', 'distortion' and partiality.[10] Hence, the distinction that some of these historians formed, when reflecting on commemoration, between history and memory. History has been defined by David Fitzpatrick as a 'dry discipline' that rejects 'appealing but flawed narratives' in favour of the truth, however 'painful and depressing' that might be.[11] Thus, it supposedly differs from memory, which approaches past events emotively through the distorting lens of the present. Underpinning such reservations about commemoration is the belief that it is both possible and necessary to distinguish between the use of the past for present-day concerns and a scholarly focus on the past for its own sake, the former of which is then associated with memory and commemorative activities, and the latter with 'professional' approaches to the past as found in the writings of trained historians. But the relationship between commemoration and history may not, in fact, be as 'contested and uneasy' as Fitzpatrick and others have suggested.[12] The form that commemoration conventionally takes – the marking of individual past events considered significant, particularly events viewed as foundational to the development of a people, nation or state – reinforces the dominant form taken by mainstream historical narratives. In the Irish context, this narrative, at its most basic, sees the history of Ireland since the beginning of the nineteenth century as a chain of events, most notably revolts and risings that posed a direct challenge to the colonial state, with lulls in between, though these revolts and risings can be framed and interpreted in quite different ways. Very little attention, comparatively speaking, is paid to the everyday forms of resistance that at times made Ireland so difficult to govern, such as the widespread refusal of men and women at various points in nineteenth- and early twentieth-century Ireland to engage with an official legal system they perceived to be unjust. Turning to the centenary of 1916, a narrow focus on the event of the Rising masked the extent to which the *de facto* 'illegal' legal and political institutions set up in its stead drew on alternative concepts and practices of legality in nineteenth- and early twentieth-century Ireland that challenged and, to varying degrees, displaced colonial institutions.[13]

The dominant historical narrative in Ireland is under-pinned by a narrow notion of the political, with events and actions only considered historically significant if they directly affect the structures of organised politics relating to the sphere of the state. History writing in Ireland has been slow to adopt a bottom-up social history of the sort that is associated with British 'history from below'.[14]

It has been equally slow to embrace the broader notion of politics that informs the writings of some post-colonial historians, most notably the group of Indian scholars who go by the title of the Subaltern Studies Collective.[15] However, over the past twenty years or so it had been making some tentative moves in these directions, as evidenced by such publications as Conor Kostick's *Revolution in Ireland* (1996), Fergus Campbell's *Land and Revolution* (2005) and my own *Subversive Law in Ireland* (2005). Will the decade of centenaries undo the conceptual reframing represented by that more recent scholarship? Will it re-establish and strengthen more traditional historical frameworks? The decade of centenaries, despite valiant attempts on the part of some individuals and groups to expand its parameters, ultimately encourages us to think about history and historical change in terms of 'key events' that are driven by 'exceptional' people.

Commemoration matters not only because of who and what it does or doesn't draw attention to but because these inclusions and omissions have consequences. State-centred history writing of the sort that is reinforced by commemoration has class and gender ramifications. The past does indeed include 'every step taken behind every plough by every peasant who has ever lived', but how many of these 'peasants' and the steps that they took made it through the selection process that is history?[16] Drawing on the language of the Decade of Centenaries website, to what extent are these steps acknowledged as constituting the 'step[s] that Ireland took'?[17] In response to these questions, it could be pointed out that not only are the rural poor often denied a place in history more generally, they are sometimes not even assigned a prominent role in discussions of events and historical periods that are quite clearly closely connected to them. An example of such an event and historical period is the Irish Land War of 1879 to 1882. While the rural poor were the momentum behind this war, in state-centred history writing the impetus for the transformations that took place in the land system in late nineteenth- and early twentieth-century Ireland is traced, in its nationalist variations, to the words and actions of the nationalist leadership, and, in its revisionist variations, to the words and actions of the colonial government. Irish nationalist and revisionist historiographies, therefore, while in some ways ideologically opposed, are both based on the assumption that the driving forces of historical change are to be found within the realm of public power.

Moreover, in historical accounts of Ireland in which the political is defined purely in terms of that which directly affects the state, and historical change is believed to be largely powered by these narrowly defined political forces, women, who were for the most part excluded from formal political culture, tend to be assigned a marginal role. State-centred histories, in other words, are invariably patriarchal histories. One of the means employed to counteract this marginalisation is to seek out examples of so-called 'exceptional' women who did operate in the arena of the state, or close to it, and focus attention on them. This strategy, which most commonly takes the form of the biographical study, could be categorised,

Figure 1: Constance Markievicz in uniform with gun. Source: National Library of Ireland [NPA MGU].

with reference to the feminist historian Gerda Lerner, as 'compensatory history', in that it is concerned with inserting 'notable women', who have 'achieved' in the same way men who are deemed 'notable' have achieved, into the 'empty spaces' of mainstream history writing.[18] While scholarship of this kind can remind us of the important role that women like Constance Markievicz played in the past in Irish society, it fails to challenge the values and structures of the history writing it is supplementing.

An historical framework that decentres familiar notions of power and the political and, consequently, expands the category of the historically relevant would automatically produce a body of scholarship more attuned to that which is at the margins of conventional history writing. It would demonstrate, for example, that everyday forms of resistance in pre-independence Ireland – the success of which required the equal participation of women and men – are as much a part of Ireland's political history as the more male-centred Rising.

In 2016 significant attempts would appear to have been made at all levels of Irish society, both official and otherwise, to incorporate women into national and local celebrations of the one hundredth anniversary of the Rising. For example, women were featured on the aforementioned commemorative coins and stamps. They were assigned a prominent place on the banners that draped Liberty Hall. Throughout the country a number of commemorative activities focused solely on women took place. Of particular note was the Cork-based Women of the South: Radicals & Revolutionaries project, which consisted of an archival photographic installation in Cork's English Market, and a series of public talks and workshops that drew attention to the range of women – feminists, nationalists, socialists, suffragists and civil-rights activists – from the Munster region of Ireland who participated in the foundation of the Irish state. The incorporation of a relatively broad range of women into the marking of an event viewed as foundational to the state has been embraced by some as signalling the advent of a more inclusive Ireland, and certainly a contrast can be formed in this regard with 'the relatively low prominence given to women' in the fiftieth commemoration of the Rising in 1966.[19] However, others have argued that the attention currently being paid to the contribution of women to the Rising has come at the cost of the neglect of the seven male signatories of the Proclamation and the sixteen men executed in the aftermath of the 1916 rebellion against British rule. Still others, more guarded in their criticisms, have not condemned the greater focus on women's involvement in the Rising as such, but have argued that the coverage of this involvement has been overly laboured at times. This critique, I would suggest, is misplaced; it is best directed not at the coverage of women's involvement in the Rising as such but at traditional historical frameworks and the stretching of them that must take place if more women are to be included in mainstream history writing. Men who 'actively' participate in the narrowly defined political domain, as did the seven members of the Irish Provisional Government, will automatically find a place in state-centred history writing. In contrast, the project of making accounts of key historical events more inclusive often involves intentionally inserting women, who may have played a crucial though less overtly 'central' role in such events,[20] into a history writing that is structurally patriarchal.

Televising the Rising

In the opening months of 2016, the five-part centenary drama *Rebellion*, broadcast on the Irish television network, RTÉ, became a focal point for discussions about women's involvement in the Rising. Amongst the fictional characters that it features are three female leads, 'ordinary' women who, if they had lived in 1916, would either have been completely omitted from the history books or consigned to a very brief footnote: Elizabeth, a medical student; May, a secretary based at Dublin Castle; and Frances, a teacher employed in Patrick Pearse's school for boys.

Marketed as a more bottom-up, woman-centred story of the Rising that told of 'ordinary people' in 'extraordinary times', *Rebellion* was both praised, at least initially, for its focus on women's contribution to this key event in Irish history and disparaged, particularly on social media, for sidelining the Rising's leaders. But the extent to which *Rebellion* is underpinned by a conventional historical framework that is anything but bottom-up and woman-centred was revealed when its writer, Colin Teevan, explained to Matt Cooper in a radio interview that he chose to place the 'protagonists' of the Rising in the background as their stories are 'well-trodden ground', and to focus instead on marginal/fictional figures whose fate is unclear.[21] Indeed, Teevan, who seemed to be defending himself against accusations made on social media that the drama was pandering to a feminist agenda, claimed that he did not start out with the intention of creating female leads. Teevan had pointed out elsewhere that he was surprised when he discovered just how many women had taken part, in various capacities, in the Rising and had sought in *Rebellion* to acknowledge their contribution.[22] However, in the interview with Cooper he stated that 'ordinary' women ended up at the centre of *Rebellion* because their very historical marginality injects a useful fresh or unknown quality into a story the audience already knows.[23] Given Teevan's assumption that this audience had been learning about the Rising from early childhood onwards, he believed it unnecessary to remind them, when writing *Rebellion*, who its key players were.[24] In other words, in the Irish context the dominant historical narrative is so pervasive, in Teevan's view, that, for dramatic purposes, it can be taken for granted.

What Cooper's interview with Teevan reveals is a tension between what I will refer to in this book, for convenience sake, as the dramatic and historic elements of historical drama, a tension that increases in direct proportion to the familiarity of the historical events being featured. The more familiar these events, the more important it is to find ways to enhance the dramatic element. The problem of how to inject a fresh or unknown quality into a story with which the audience is very familiar also clearly arose with *Insurrection*, a docu-drama shown on RTÉ on the golden jubilee of the Rising. However, in the case of *Insurrection* this problem was largely dealt with through formal techniques. The year 1966 was the first time that a majority of Irish households owned a television set. Ireland's premier television channel was still relatively new, having only begun broadcasting on New Year's Eve 1961, and *Insurrection* famously drew heavily on its not excessive financial and technical resources. Indeed, the *RTÉ Guide* for the week described it as 'undoubtedly the most difficult and ambitious project ever attempted by Irish television'.[25] The script, written by Hugh Leonard, was inspired by Max Caulfield's *The Easter Rebellion*, a 1964 narrative account of the Rising based on eye-witness testimonies. The premise of *Insurrection* is that the events of the Rising are being filmed and reported on as they take place, thereby making the Rising seem current, chaotic and unpredictable.[26] On-the-spot reporters interview participants and bystanders, while camera crews gather footage from key locations, mostly, though not exclusively, in Dublin city. On occasions the filming itself became chaotic as actual bystanders tried to intervene in the action to comment on discrepancies between the events, as they remembered them or had been informed of them, and how they were being portrayed![27] *Insurrection* featured a large cast of actors, some of whom delivered quite amateurish performances. Ray McNally was a notable exception in this regard. He ably played a studio news anchor who is clearly quite taken aback by proceedings, but gallantly attempts to uncover, explain and link together the surprising events that are happening around him in Ireland:

What is the connection between this newspaper item [with Eoin MacNeill's countermanding order] and certain startling events off the Kerry coast? This evening we take a close look at Sinn Féin and we ask ourselves what is this organisation? Who are its leaders? And why have the Government not taken action against them for treasonable activities? Parades, marches and so-called manoeuvres are one thing but consorting and planning with the Germans is quite another. Strong words? Well, we shall see.[28]

The opening episode from which these words are taken was first shown on Easter Sunday 1966. The drama ran over eight consecutive nights, taking the form of a thirty-minute news report covering through 'live' footage, reportage and commentary – often aided by models and maps – the events of the Rising that had occurred that day. The result is an odd but interesting conflation of time periods; the events being reported on are supposedly taking place in 1916 and are being reported on as they happen, but very little attempt is made to disguise the fact that the reporting is being conducted in the 1960s.

This formal aspect of *Insurrection* defamiliarises the Rising by presenting it from the perspective of a news crew who are closely observing it but, despite their 1960s attire and technical trappings, do not know how it will end. Indeed, the 'news report' that concludes with the evacuation of the GPO is titled 'Do you think we'll win?'. Consequently, those watching, even members of the audience who have an in-depth knowledge of this period of Irish history, are encouraged to engage

Figure 2: *Insurrection*: reporter in modern clothes. Source: RTÉ Archives.

in counterfactual historical speculation on what could potentially happen next. The Taoiseach of Ireland in 1966 was Seán Lemass, who is often uncritically celebrated, alongside the economist T.K. Whitaker, for spearheading Ireland's transformation from a financial backwater into a 'modern' country with an outward-looking economy.[29] For Lemass, the fiftieth anniversary of the Rising was 'a time of national stocktaking, and for trying to look ahead into the mists of the future to see the right road leading to the high destiny we desire for our nation'.[30] However, *Insurrection*, in its very form, suggests that the present is open-ended, even if the present that it portrays is in the past; though itself chronologically linear, this early drama features a past present that could potentially lead to many 'right' roads.

A very different approach is taken in *Rebellion*. Formally far less innovative than *Insurrection* and, in terms of plot emphasis and development, closer to *Downton Abbey* than RTÉ's earlier commemoratory drama, it deals with the tension between the dramatic and historic elements of historical drama purely through character by introducing the audience to three fictional women who have been caught up, in one case unwittingly, in the events of 1916. By way of these women – Elizabeth, May and Frances – Teevan sought to take 'a story leading to an end we all know' in 'surprising ways'.[31] The principal function of these women, therefore, is to ensure that an audience familiar with the Rising will still be compelled to find out what happens next, though in this case such speculation is for the most part restricted to the personal lives of the drama's fictional characters. For example, in the early episodes of *Rebellion* May is in an illicit relationship with Charles Hammond, a married Dublin Castle civil servant who has a history of forming temporary, and largely exploitative, relationships with 'native' women in whatever colonial territory he happens to be based. During the course of the series she becomes pregnant. Her fate and that of her baby provides a cliff hanger ending to the first series. Indeed, it is one of the principal unknowns that links this drama to the sequel that RTÉ has since commissioned on the War of Independence. Thus, while *Rebellion* in its focus on 'ordinary' women might appear, on initial assessment, to challenge mainstream historical narratives, the personal stories of its female leads provide no real threat to such narratives or the frameworks that facilitate them. Indeed, what Cooper's interview with Teevan ultimately indicates is that *Rebellion*, in keeping with commemorative practices more generally, developed out of the assumption that history is comprised of key events driven by exceptional people. In the case of the Rising, however, Teevan judged these historical figures to be so exceptional that their stories do not even require retelling.

Remembering Past Futures

In the remainder of this book I will outline and advocate a new approach to commemoration. In place of marking individual past occurrences considered significant in mainstream versions of history, I suggest that we seek out and 'remember' the roads untaken. Commemoration of this kind involves a radical reconceptualisation of history. To seek out and 'remember' the roads untaken, we must not only reject state-centred history writing, we must also challenge the temporal lens through which historical events are typically viewed. In conventional history writing the past tends to be read backwards. As previously outlined here, the past overlaps with history, but is not the same as history in that not all of the past is transformed into history; indeed, most of what happens in the past is considered too peripheral and insignificant to make it through the selection process that is history. The philosopher and cultural critic Walter Benjamin quite rightly claimed that a past moment becomes 'historical posthumously, as it were, through events that may be separated from it by thousands of years'.[32] Thus, the events, ideas, groupings and individuals that receive most attention in history writing are not only those that operated within a narrowly defined political arena but those that are believed to have had the most impact on what happened afterwards. The implicit starting point is the present. The primary focus of attention is that which has most obviously led to *this* point in time. The present is thereby made to seem inevitable, a preordained destiny towards which the past has been resolutely and transparently travelling. This backwards approach to history was parodied by George Russell, also known as Æ, at a dinner party in 1914:

The small holdings of the nineteenth and twentieth centuries gradually come into the hands of the large owners, in the eighteenth century progress has been made and the first glimmerings of self-government appear, religious troubles and wars follow until the last Englishman, Strongbow, leaves the country, culture begins, religious intolerance ceases with the disappearance of Patrick, about AD 400, and we approach the great age of the heroes and gods.[33]

While Russell's explicit target here was clearly narrow-gauge nationalist history writing, particularly in its more myth-inflected variations, his parody has a much broader applicability in that it is relevant to all seamlessly progressive histories in which it is made to seem as if one thing simply led to another until we reached *our* point in time.

But what if we approached the past differently? What if we viewed each moment in time as a moment of possibility, while recognising that some time periods are particularly potent with possibility? A passage from James Joyce's *Ulysses*, written during the decade Ireland is currently commemorating, paves the way for this more radical approach to history:

> Had Pyrrhus not fallen by a beldam's hand in Argos or Julius Caesar not been knifed to death. They are not to be thought away. Time has branded them and fettered they are lodged in the room of the infinite possibilities they have ousted. But can those have been possible seeing that they never were? Or was that only possible which came to pass?[34]

'Branded', 'fettered', 'lodged': a language of servitude, slavery and entrapment is used in this passage to describe the process via which the selective narrativisation of the past that is history can seal the fate of its material. In petrifying the past, history not only suppresses alternative versions of the events that happened but closes off the stories of what else might have been.

This *Ulysses* extract not only conjures up the notion of alternative pasts but encourages us to speculate on the potential futures that could have resulted from those pasts. But how do we access alternative pasts and the futures they could have given rise to? We must first reject unilinear models of history that approach a past moment as if its future were singular as opposed to potentially multiple. We must then broaden our focus beyond the events, ideas, groupings and individuals that are now perceived from our present standpoint as being the most significant. As Paul K. Saint-Amour proposes in *Tense Future*, we must cast 'lateral shadows' on a given moment, illuminating the roads 'that branched off to the side, as it were, of how events actually unfolded'.[35] In other words, we must engage in counterfactual thinking, considering not only what happened but what else might conceivably have happened. By acknowledging the existence of historical alternatives at a given moment in time we can access that moment's contingencies: unrealised yet possible past futures. In the aforementioned passage Stephen Dedalus poses the following question: 'was that only possible which came to pass?'[36] In response I would suggest that these side-branching roads were often no less likely for having been untaken by events.

Periods of Potent Possibility

But was the decade that Ireland is currently commemorating, the ten years leading up to and just after the
establishment of the Free State, a period of potent possibility? Moreover, how is such a period best defined?
Since the beginning of the decade of centenaries commentators have quite rightly pointed to the openness
of these ten years to interpretation. They have drawn
attention to its varied legacies.[37] These multiple and
often contradictory legacies, I would suggest, are a
direct result of the time period's multiple untaken roads.
At each and every instant of time, however brief, there
are, of course, numerous roads that branch off to the
side of how events actually unfold. During periods of
potent possibility, these untaken roads are particularly
abundant. W.B. Yeats' poem 'Easter 1916', with its fam-
ous refrain 'All changed, changed utterly / A terrible
beauty is born', is often cited when claims are made as
to the transformative impact of the Rising.[38] The poem's
form, which alludes to the exact date of the beginning
of the Rising, pinpoints with precision the moment of
this perceived change; as Clair Wills points out, 'The
poem consists of four stanzas, alternating between sixteen and twenty-four lines: 24/4/16'.[39] Less frequently
the following assertion by Yeats is taken as representative of the impact of the Rising on the Irish mentality:
'As yet one knows nothing of the future except that it
must be very unlike the past'.[40] These Yeats extracts
could be read alongside Stephen Gwynn's 1918 nostalgic

recollections of pre-Rising Ireland to indicate that the Rising itself had resulted in a dramatic transformation in how Irish people perceived themselves and their place in the world. Gwynn, a constitutional nationalist, reminisced about 'those who lived more easily and quietly in the Ireland of yesterday, and held with an unquestioning spirit to the state of things in which they were born'.[41] I would suggest, however, that these sentiments could just as easily have been penned before the Rising as after it. Indeed, it is relatively easy to find similar assertions of a transforming world that date from the period running up to the Rising. For example, prior to this event, Arthur Griffith, writing under a pen name in the monthly feminist journal *Bean na hÉireann*, dramatically declared that Ireland was ready for a 'gynocracy ... I am weary living in a world ruled by men with mouse-hearts and monkey-brains and I want change'.[42] Indeed, as early as 1905 the Cork nationalist Liam de Róiste wrote in his diary of both his and Ireland's current state of flux:

> I often wonder whether there has been an actual, objective change of affairs, or of general ideas in Ireland during the past decade that makes things seem different to me now from what they did three, four, five years ago. Or, is it a change of ideas within myself, the inevitable change from boyhood to youth, from youth to manhood? I presume both are working. I am changing and things around me change.[43]

Periods of potent possibility are characterised by a prevailing belief – often connected to the collapse of dominant socio-political formations or ideologies, such as the demise, for example, of Irish landlordism – that the future can be very different from the present and that it can be shaped by those living in that present. They are points in time in which it is believed that anything could and, in fact, might happen. Thus, while such time periods can give rise to the kinds of events that become the focus of both state-centred history writing and commemorative activities, such events are only one aspect of these time periods. Indeed, what differentiates periods of potent possibility from other points in time is their openness, the very real possibility that these events could easily have been supplanted by other events that would have been assigned equal weight in the history books. However, this openness tends to be masked upon the rise to dominance of a new political formation or ideology, the success of which is largely reliant upon it presenting all that went before it as that which led up to it. In this manner the historical openness that characterises moments of possibility can end up being subsumed into a narrative of historical development.

Counterfactualism

Perhaps not surprisingly, periods of potent possibility can give rise to a greater number of fictional works that contain counterfactual elements. Indeed, this is one of the ways that the historical openness of these time periods may become evident to a later generation whose initial encounter with such points of time is shaped by a latterly imposed narrative of historical development. In 1922, the same year that Stephen Dedalus' counterfactual historical speculations appeared in print in *Ulysses*, a considerably less well-known though no less experimental and ambitious text was first performed: a sequence of plays titled *Back to Methuselah* by George Bernard Shaw. *Back to Methuselah* – which Shaw judged unperformable on stage[44] but nonetheless considered his masterpiece – is generally interpreted against the backdrop of the First World War; the five plays and substantial preface that comprise this work were clearly prompted by the devastation of that war in that the text looks to a future when statesmen have discovered 'that cowardice [is] a great patriotic virtue', and humans live long enough to fully grasp the futility of war.[45] Indeed, following the destruction of all the capital cities of the world in the war that followed the 'war called the War to end War', these statesmen become such disciples of the doctrine of cowardice that they erect a statue in commemoration of 'its first preacher, an ancient and very fat sage called Sir John Falstaff'![46] However, a less overt context for *Back to Methuselah* is suggested by the initial setting of the penultimate play: in the year AD 3000 on 'Burrin [*sic*] pier on the south shore of Galway Bay in Ireland, a region of stone-capped hills and granite fields'.[47]

The opening pages of this very odd play sequence centre on the assertion that 'everything is possible:

everything'.[48] These words are spoken by The Serpent, interestingly established as female, to Eve in the Garden of Eden in this science-fiction fantasy that spans the ages from Adam and Eve to a projected superhuman world some thirty millennia into the future. A former atheist turned self-professed mystic, Shaw defines a miracle, via the voice of The Serpent, as 'an impossible thing that is nevertheless possible. Something that never could happen, and yet does happen.'[49] Eve later – or, more specifically, a few centuries later – tells Adam and Cain of her 'hope' of 'the coming true of your dreams and mine', informing them that 'the serpent said that every dream could be willed into creation by those strong enough to believe in it'.[50] In this text the man who takes pride in not only 'seeing things as they are' but having 'the power of imagining things as they are, even when I cannot see them' is a warmonger, a latter-day Cain, who is responsible for 'the shedding of oceans of blood, the death of millions of men'.[51] In keeping with the utopian bent of the text,[52] *Back to Methuselah* contains a passage that is arguably the most heavily quoted and paraphrased counterfactual statement of all time: 'I hear you say "Why?" Always "Why?" You see things; and you say "Why?" But I dream things that never were; and I say "Why not?"'[53] These lines were most famously paraphrased by John F. Kennedy during his 1963 visit to Ireland, but this Shaw passage was also a favourite of Robert Kennedy's. It was adopted by him in his presidential-campaign speeches in the spring of 1968. Indeed, following Robert Kennedy's assassination,

Edward Kennedy used these words to close a eulogy for his dead brother. In hindsight the incorporation of the Shaw passage into this particular eulogy seems apt, as, in the aftermath of his death, Robert Kennedy has become the subject of so many counterfactual thought experiments. He is the figure at the core of the 'what ifs' of North American politics. What if Robert Kennedy had survived and gone on to beat Richard Nixon in the 1968 presidential election? What would this have meant for internal American politics? What would it have meant for world politics? Here counterfactual thinking overlaps with the great man theory of history; historical change, this theory holds, is largely attributable to the impact of exceptional individuals, invariably male. In Ireland we have had our own versions of that combination in the more mainstream counterfactual speculations on the period we are currently commemorating. Such speculations tend to be restricted to asking how the course of Irish history might have been different if one or another of the condemned leaders of the Rising had evaded execution and gone on to shape Free State Ireland.

In a 2014 article Juan F. Elices claims that Ireland has produced very few examples of literary texts that, through counterfactualism, 'seek to undermine some long-standing and unquestioned historical assumptions'.[54] However, literary works that encourage counterfactual thinking do not have to be counterfactual fiction as conventionally understood. The most fertile ground for literary counterfactual thought experiments is arguably Nazism; Len Deighton's *SS-GB* (1978) and

Robert Harris' *Fatherland* (1992) are two of the better known novels that construct the world that follows the defeat of the Allies by Nazi Germany in the Second World War, while Philip Roth's *The Plot Against America* (2004) imagines a scenario whereby Charles Lindbergh wins the presidential election of 1940 and signs a treaty with Nazi Germany, heralding a period of heightened anti-Semitism in North America. But literary counter-factualism is not only comprised of alternative histories in which certain alternations in past events considered key in mainstream history writing result in a present that is very different to our own. In Shaw's play sequence *Back to Methuselah*, the play that is set in the present of the text's conception, 'the first years after the war of 1914–18',[55] is, in fact, the present as Shaw knew it, but a fringe or marginal element in this present, not perceived at the time as having any great importance, is shown to be the foundation for a future that is unimaginable to most in that present: 'if the Accountant General will go to the British Museum library, and search the catalogue, he will find ... a curious and now forgotten book, dated 1924, entitled *The Gospel of the Brothers Barnabas*. That gospel was that men must live three hundred years if civilisation is to be saved.'[56] In *Back to Methuselah* this 'gospel' – which is dismissed by most of the contemporaries of the Barnabas brothers as outlandish or, at best, improbable – is a side-branching road that eventually becomes the new norm. Literary texts that encourage counterfactual thinking, therefore, can simply be works of fiction that cast lateral shadows.

Joyce has received considerable attention from scholars who have an interest in literary works that contain this counterfactual feature – side-shadowing – though relatively little attention is paid in this scholarship to the relationship between the counterfactual elements of Joyce's writings and the period of history that we are now commemorating in Ireland. Nevertheless, these writings have been cited by scholars as examples of 'structural counterfactualism'; texts whose 'form models the future's openness'.[57] Neither *Dubliners* nor *Ulysses* centre on 'the life story of a single, clearly identifiable protagonist',[58] though the first three episodes of *Ulysses* play with the reader's expectation that this text will continue on from *A Portrait of the Artist as a Young Man*, offering a further instalment in the life of Stephen Dedalus. When taken in its entirety, however, rather than presenting us with a protagonist, *Ulysses*, like *Dubliners*, protagonises a whole city and historical point in time.[59] Moreover, the foreground of each of these texts is densely populated with multiple subjects and collectivities. In their very form, therefore, both point to a variety of possible futures. This is particularly the case with *Ulysses*, a text that features not only multiple subjects but countless near encounters between these subjects. For example, the tenth episode of *Ulysses* details the simultaneous movements of nearly all of the novel's characters, significant and minor, through Dublin over a one-hour period, showing how they nearly cross paths on a number of occasions: 'On Newcomen bridge the very reverend John Conmee S.J. of saint

Francis Xavier's church, upper Gardiner street, stepped on to an outward bound tram. Off an inward bound tram stepped the reverend Nicholas Dudley C.C. of saint Agatha's church, north William street, on to Newcomen bridge.'[60] The title of this episode, 'Wandering Rocks', is a reference to the road untaken in Homer's *The Odyssey*: the route that Odysseus does not follow back to Ithaca. The meetings that could take place between characters in *Ulysses* but either don't or are significantly delayed are a constant reminder of the potential of the story to develop otherwise. While Shaw's *Back to Methuselah* is formally quite different to the aforementioned writings by Joyce, it likewise casts lateral shadows. Moreover, *Back to Methuselah* and *Ulysses* are shaped by equally odd temporalities: *Ulysses*, which takes place over the course of one day, is notable for its unusual temporal squatness, while *Back to Methuselah*, which traces humankind from its origins to 'as far as thought can reach', is characterised by a distinctive temporal stretch.

Progressivism

Counterfactual thinking of the kind that is voiced by Stephen Dedalus in *Ulysses* and Shaw's serpent in *Back to Methuselah* – literary texts written and published during the decade we are currently commemorating in Ireland – poses a challenge to an historical approach that claims to record past events 'wie es eigentlich gewesen' [as they really were].[61] Leopold von Ranke, a German historian who is generally viewed as the founder of modern 'professional' history writing, famously asserted that the principal task of the historian was to uncover 'what actually happened'. For Ranke and those who take their inspiration from him, 'the past should be studied in its own moral frame of reference and things ought always to be seen in their own historical context, without the judgement of hindsight'.[62] However, notwithstanding an idealised notion of the discipline as an objective, indeed scientific, 'presentation of the facts',[63] the 'professional' history writing that views itself as the heir of this nineteenth-century philosophy does not merely provide useful information about past events, it inevitably endows these events with significance and meaning. As David Scott points out in *Conscripts of Modernity*, 'there is no single way in which the history of an event … can be told. That the history of an event … gets written in one way rather than another, that the sequence of recorded actions gets cast in this way rather than that, cannot be simply read off from the historical facts by themselves.'[64] Vantage point is always a factor in how a past event does actually get narrated. For all of its assertions of impartiality, conventional history writing tends to be aligned with dominant groupings in contemporary society. It might proclaim sympathy for the casualties of the past, but, as Walter Benjamin pointed out in his theses on the philosophy of history, it invariably empathises with the victors and their present-day counterparts, 'the heirs of prior conquerors'.[65]

That said, history is not always the product of a straightforward process in which some are victorious and, consequently, have their voices heard, and some lose out and, therefore, have no representative voice; an additional point that could be added to Benjamin's claims is that not all casualties of the past are treated equally in mainstream history writing. For example, while strong similarities can be drawn in the Irish context between the fate of agricultural labourers and the fate of landlords, the demise of the former grouping has received far less scholarly attention than that of the latter. As Gearóid Ó Tuathaigh points out, 'for the landless agricultural labourers, the nineteenth-century answer to their particular land question was a brutal, unambiguous "exit"'.[66] First decimated by the Famine, changing land practices in the post-Famine period, in particular an expansion in grazing, 'rendered them increasingly surplus to requirements'.[67] Moreover, agricultural labourers gained little under land reform and redistribution. Some casual rural workers were still selling their labour in hiring fairs in Donegal and elsewhere well into the twentieth century, and agitating for better pay and conditions. However, by the second half of the nineteenth century emigration was one of the few remaining viable options for this grouping as a whole. Through emigration the rural poor of Ireland became the urban proletariat of Britain and elsewhere, contradictorily characterised as both an obstacle to class struggle and key players in the most revolutionary working-class movements.[68] Irish landlords, the grouping at the apex as opposed to the base of the rural pyramid, likewise largely passed out of Irish history in the latter part of the Union era, erased as a class by land reform. However, as Ó Tuathaigh states, their prolonged retreat is the focus of a markedly elegiac body of scholarship, a 'thriving research industry on Irish landed estates and the world of the Big House and its past occupants'.[69]

For Ó Tuathaigh this discrepancy in scholarly attention is partially attributable to the fact that, notwithstanding the achievements of such figures as Peadar O'Donnell and Patrick MacGill, the demise of the landlords was much more 'richly documented' than that of the landless agricultural labourers.[70] It may also be relevant that cultural artefacts were a key component of this documentation. According to Benjamin, those who participate 'in the triumphal procession in which current rulers step over those who are lying prostrate' carry 'spoils' more commonly referred to as 'cultural treasures'.[71] Benjamin was referring here to the way in which the social forces that brought the capitalist world into being legitimised their victory by virtue of their nurturing and guardianship of culture. In the Irish context many of the items that we now consider 'cultural treasures' are linked, even if only tentatively, to Irish landlordism. This link enhances the nostalgia that tinges accounts of the landlords' exit from Irish history. The guardianship of such 'cultural treasures' by current dominant groupings in Irish society justifies their dominant position. Venerated cultural works, traditionally viewed as separate from the world at large, are referred to by Benjamin as 'spoils' in that he believed they are as much a product of the labour of those who have been stepped over, the casualties of the past, as of either those who made them or those who take part in the victory procession and claim them to look after them: 'They owe their existence not only to the efforts of the great geniuses who created them, but also to the anonymous toil of others who lived in the same period.'[72] This 'anonymous toil' includes the work of Irish landless agricultural labourers. Consequently, while items viewed as art are hallowed by an 'aura' of beauty, culture, in Benjamin's opinion, is invariably bound up with a history of exploitation and oppression. Thus, he maintained, in his most oft-quoted line, that 'there is no document of civilisation which is not at the same time a document of barbarism'.[73] As pointed out by a more recent commentator, Paul K. Saint-Amour, the barbarism that Benjamin referred to in 'Theses on the Philosophy of History' is elided by a Whig history writing underpinned by a seamless progressivism: 'no sooner does such a historicism recover lost acts, experiences, and subjects than it reincorporates them into a progressive model of history, one that consecrates the violence of the rulers as law and forgets the barbarism involved in the production of their cultural treasures'.[74]

James Connolly, one of the signatories of the Proclamation declaring an Irish Republic, fully grasped the extent to which progressivism serves a ruling-class presentism. Connolly, who following his execution in 1916 was turned into a 'conventional nationalist with

Figure 3: James Connolly on the window of the Brown Thomas department store. Source: Ronan McGreevy.

a slight red streak',[75] is himself a reminder of the dangers of a mainstream history writing that reads events, ideas, groupings and individuals backwards and through a narrowly defined political lens. The prominent placing of a poster of this labour activist and Marxist theorist of decolonisation on the window of the Dublin branch of Brown Thomas to commemorate the Rising is responsible for arguably the single most ironic image produced by Ireland's decade of centenaries thus far.

That an image of Connolly ended up adorning an upmarket clothing chain that specialises in what its website refers to as exclusive or luxury brands should not be at all surprising, however. Shortly after his death Connolly was co-opted by Irish bourgeois nationalism as a potent symbol of its struggle. By the late 1920s the containment of Connolly in the image of 'nationalist martyr' was so complete that Éamon de Valera could assert that 'his political positions were closer to Connolly's than to any other figure in the republican tradition'.[76] As Gregory Dobbins points out, 'such statements gauged not only the manner by which an emergent Fianna Fáil redirected the political sympathies of a substantial portion of the population away from the democratic socialism of the Labour Party towards its own more generally populist brand of nationalism, but also the extent to which Connolly's radicalism had been muted' in the remaking of him as a national icon.[77]

In recent years James Connolly has been quite rightly reclaimed by Dobbins, David Lloyd, Conor McCarthy and others as one of Ireland's most radical thinkers and activists.[78] An early pamphlet titled *Erin's Hope* has played a key role in this reappraisal of Connolly. In this 1897 pamphlet Connolly commented on the ideological function served by progressivism, claiming that so-called 'progressive ideas' are aligned with, and uphold, 'the present order of society'.[79] Hence, Connolly, in his theorisation of land and landholding in Ireland, looked back to look forwards. In the opening pages of *Erin's Hope* Connolly claimed that pre-Conquest Ireland had been

inspired by the democratic principle that property was intended to serve the people, and not by the principle so universally acted upon at present, viz. that the people have no other function in existing than to be the bondslaves of those who by force or by fraud have managed to possess themselves of property.[80]

Indeed, according to Connolly common ownership of land or a 'primitive communism' that in other countries had failed to acquire 'a higher status than that conferred by the social sanction of unlettered and uneducated tribes' had in Ireland

formed part of the well defined social organisations of a nation of scholars and students, recognised by Chief and Tanist, Brehon and Bard, as the inspiring principle of their collective life, and the basis of their national system of jurisprudence.[81]

For Connolly, therefore, common ownership of land in pre-colonial Ireland could potentially provide a basis for a future system of non-exploitative landholding in an independent Ireland. In championing that which could emerge from what others had dismissed as a primitive system of landholding, Connolly was offering a strong challenge to progressivist thinking:

The ardent student of sociology, who believes that the progress of the human race through the various stages of communism, chattel slavery, feudalism and wage slavery, has been but a preparation for the higher ordered society of the future ... will perhaps regard the Irish adherence to clan ownership at such a comparatively recent date as the seventeenth century as evidence of a retarded economic development, and therefore a real hindrance to progress. But the sympathetic student of history, who believes in the

possibility of a people by political intuition anticipat-
ing the lessons afterwards revealed to them in the sad
school of experience, will not be indisposed to join
with the ardent Irish patriot in his lavish expressions
of admiration for the sagacity of his Celtic forefathers,
who foreshadowed in the democratic organisation of
the Irish clan the more perfect organisation of the
free society of the future.[82]

Connolly is central to the decade of centenaries, but
his celebration of disparaged ways of thinking and being has garnered no attention in the official programme
of commemorations. In a radical commemorative process that seeks to reanimate the social imagination by
'remembering' ideas and practices that challenge current
orthodoxies, this aspect of Connolly would be key.

LAND[83]

However, while Connolly should be reclaimed and commemorated as one of the more revolutionary voices of
the first half of the decade we are currently marking in
Ireland, it is also important to acknowledge that he was
not writing in a vacuum. Land nationalisation, as previously envisaged by Michael Davitt, was a precursor to
Connolly's Gaelic communism.[84] Davitt was hostile to a
landlord system he associated with both feudalism and
colonialism. However, he sought a viable alternative not
only to a pro-British unionism intent on integrating

Ireland more fully into the British capitalist economy, but also to an anti-colonial nationalism that sought to reproduce the conditions of that economy on Irish soil. Though accusing landlordism of impeding 'the march of progress', Davitt was keen to differentiate his conception as to the direction this march should take from the vision of those who sought to transform Ireland into a modern capitalist nation.[85] At the first Land League convention Davitt read from a document he claimed embodied the principles and rules of this new association. Landlordism, he proclaimed, was a 'feudal idea' that 'came in with the conquest'. 'Associated with foreign dominion', it 'has never to this day been recognised by the moral sentiments of the people'. Consequently, 'for the protection of the proprietorial rights of a few thousand landlords in the country, a standing army of semi-military police is maintained'.[86] In Davitt's analysis the land system as it operated in nineteenth-century Ireland was most accurately categorised as feudal. However, he also sought to demonstrate that this feudal system had been imposed through conquest and, consequently, was quite distinct to feudalism as it had been experienced in England. In *The Fall of Feudalism in Ireland* Davitt provided the following assessment of Irish landlordism: 'Property has its duties under the feudal system of tenure, as well as its rights, but in Ireland those enjoying the monopoly of the land have only considered that they had rights, and have always been forgetful of their duties.'[87] The 'march of progress' that Davitt advocated would not simply replace this flawed feudalism with rural capitalism but would seek to interpret contemporary agrarian radicalism in the context of Ireland's experience of colonialism. Reiterating John Stuart Mill's belief that 'before the conquest, the Irish people knew nothing of absolute property in land', Davitt argued that it was possible to find traces of communal land ownership in contemporary rural practices.[88] It was these traces that would form the basis of a system of land nationalisation capable of providing an alternative to both feudal and capitalist concepts of property. The application of the notion of a 'march of progress' to that of collective property rights implies that, for Davitt, it was not simply a matter of turning back the clock. In Davitt's analysis an older concept of land ownership still existed in a contemporary form, even if only a fringe or marginal element in Irish society. This could be merged with an enlightened politics to create a side-branching road that ultimately led to a fairer land system.

Davitt's writings suggest that there was a contemporary context and impetus for the more radical conceptualisations of land usage put forward in the period running up to, and during, the decade we are currently commemorating in Ireland. This contemporary context and impetus was agrarian agitation. What an analysis of such agitation reveals is that the struggle over land in late nineteenth- and early twentieth-century Ireland was shaped as much by assertions of rights of occupancy as by rights of ownership in the narrow sense of this term. Donal J. O'Sullivan, in his history of Irish policing from 1822 to 1922, describes the 'fishing of privately owned rivers and lakes and hunting over ground which was privately owned or preserved' as a common feature of the Land War period.[89] Interestingly, those arrested for 'poaching' sometimes made the case that they had a perfect right to hunt the land having been given permission to do so by the tenant farmers who occupied it, the tenant-farmers' rights of occupancy clearly taking precedence, in their view, over the landlords' rights of ownership. On 28 November 1881 the *Freeman's Journal* reported on an 'extraordinary affair' that took place on the property of Dowager Lady Massy. Five tenant farmers caught 'poaching' on this property with greyhounds were prosecuted and fined, but returned later with a large body of men and proceeded to hunt in full view of the gamekeeper and his assistants. According to the *Freeman's Journal*, 'an immense amount of damage was done, and a large number of game killed' as a result of this defiant behaviour.[90] In a letter to the editor of the *Freeman's Journal* the following week, one of the 'poachers' present on the day in question sought to establish a different framework through which his activities could be interpreted. In this alternative version of events, five men did indeed go onto Dowager Lady Massy's property with dogs for the purpose of hunting, but they had a 'perfect right' to be there 'having got permission from the tenants thereon'. When the gamekeeper 'accosted us and told us the lands were preserved, and not to hunt on them', the men were on land occupied by Thomas Byrne, who had 'invited us to hunt on his farm'. The men informed the gamekeeper that 'we had leave to hunt from the tenant, who was present, and who told us to hunt away as long as we wished to. The gamekeeper took down our names to summon us, but we did not mind but hunted away' as 'fines had no right to be imposed on us'.[91] George Bernard Shaw – who, like Davitt, was a proponent of land nationalisation – was perhaps inspired by such present-day conceptual clashes regarding land and its usages when penning the following futuristic passage for *Back to Methuselah*:

> The Woman ... Why are you here?
>
> The Elderly Gentleman. Am I trespassing? I was not aware of it.
>
> The Woman. Trespassing? I do not understand the word.
>
> The Elderly Gentleman. Is this land private property? If so, I make no claim. I proffer a shilling in satisfaction of damage (if any), and am ready to withdraw if you will be good enough to show me the nearest way. [*He offers her a shilling.*]
>
> The Woman [*taking it and examining it without much interest*]. I do not understand a single word of what you have just said.[92]

Landlord tenant relations in the period leading up to the decade we are currently commemorating in Ireland were characterised by a widespread refusal by tenant farmers to recognise the absolute property rights of the landlord class. This refusal was evidenced by both the manner in which the tenant farmer defined his/her relationship to the land and more active forms of protest, such as resistance to a landlord's attempt to sell, lease, evict and hunt as he/she pleased. The land Act that William Gladstone introduced in 1881 during his second administration was both a response to this widespread refusal and an attempt to provide a legal framework for the de facto relationship between the Irish tenant farmer and the land he/she occupied.

Gladstone's measures, however, altered the law in ways that even some members of his own government feared would interfere with accepted British legal principles, particularly in relation to the inviolability of the rights of property.[93] As Philip Bull points out in his study of the Irish land question, the social and political model that embodied these principles was relatively straightforward:

> the 'owners' of the land are indeed its owners in absolute terms, with the right to sell or lease as they pleased and at whatever price allowed by the market. Any interference with these 'property rights' was anathema – property being central and sacred to the 'old society' and to the new capitalist order emerging in its place.[94]

Thus, the English author Anthony Trollope, fearful of the implications of such interference, interrupted the storyline of his 1883 Irish novel *The Landleaguers* on a number of occasions to comment on what he referred to as the misguided desire of some members of the Liberal

Party to put 'up a new law devised by themselves in lieu of that time-honoured law by which property has ever been protected in England'.[95] Trollope was not alone in feeling compelled to argue that to interfere with the market was to 'attempt to alter the laws for governing the world'.[96] The Conservative peer Lord Salisbury – who had previously predicted that an assault on property rights would begin in Ireland and then spread to England, Scotland and Wales – described Gladstone as a madman who had abrogated property rights in the misguided hope that he could reduce the hatred of the Irish for England.[97]

The first major Irish land Act put through Parliament, the Landlord and Tenant Law Amendment Act, 1860 – also known as Deasy's Act – had sought to assimilate Irish agriculture to English models. The anomalous nature of Irish land relations was to be 'regulated' through the abolition of customary tenant right and the enforcement of absolute rights of ownership as vested in the landlord. This Act, described by Philip Bull as 'the "last hurrah" of the confident English assumption that the spirit of Irish native culture could be subdued to the letter of British law and the tenets of British economic ideology', clarified the contractual nature of landlord–tenant relations and strengthened the power of the landlord in many areas, including eviction.[98]

Gladstone, when introducing a subsequent land bill to the House of Commons in 1870, adopted a contrasting approach. He claimed that while in England and Scotland 'the idea of holding land by contract is perfectly traditional and familiar to the mind of every man', in Ireland,

where the old Irish ideas were never supplanted except by the rude hand of violence – by laws written on
the statute book, but never entering into the heart of
the Irish people – the people have not generally embraced the idea of the occupation of land by contract;
and the old Irish notion that some interest in the soil
adheres to the tenant, even though his contract has
expired, is everywhere rooted in the popular mind.[99]

The land Acts of 1870 and 1881 recognised the rights of
occupancy that the Irish tenant farmer believed he/she
had to the land, rights that had been asserted through
acts of agrarian agitation. However, such rights were
in contradiction to the absolute rights of ownership
vested in landlordism under Deasy's Act. Consisting of
a series of measures specifically designed to monitor
the relationship between landlord and tenant, these
later Acts were feared by many to have fundamentally
breached British conceptions of property law and rights.
Under the 1881 land Act, for example, rent was no longer fixed by the market but by special tribunals, the
landlord's right to evict was restricted, and the tenant
farmer was allowed to sell his/her 'interest' in the holding. In reaction to this violation of property concepts,
Conservative policy-makers, concerned that ambiguous
property relations in Ireland could create a precedent
that would unsettle concepts of property on mainland
Britain, began to look to land-purchase schemes as the
only possible solution.[100] The unacceptable interference
with property that they believed had been enshrined in

the 1881 Act had to be dismantled. If, in the Irish context, landlords could not hold absolute property rights, ownership of the land would have to be transferred to the tenant farmers who cultivated it. By the mid-1880s key figures within the Conservative Party were convinced that the creation of a peasant proprietary class was the sole means through which Irish property rights could be clarified. Consequently, it was the British political party that claimed to represent 'landlordism' that set in motion a series of land-purchase Acts designed to bring about an inversion in land ownership in Ireland, thus revealing that they valued absolute property rights above loyalty to any particular grouping. Under the first of these Acts, the Ashbourne Act of 1885, tenants could obtain loans for the full amount of the purchase price of their holdings, repayable in a period of forty-nine years by an annuity of four per cent per annum. These guidelines contrasted favourably to the purchase clauses contained in the 1881 land Act that had required the tenant to raise a quarter of the purchase money on his/her own to be paid back in thirty-five years with an annual rate of five per cent. The 1885 land Act was intended, therefore, to appeal strongly to tenant farmers who might be considering buying the property they cultivated, and, consequently, to speed the transfer of ownership of land in Ireland. The half a million acres that changed hands during its first three years of operation suggests that, in this regard, the Act should be counted a success.

However, in the years following these Acts there were intermittent reports from around the country of land, particularly grazing land, being seized by groups of labourers and small farmers. This agrarian agitation culminated in the land seizures or so-called 'agrarian Bolshevism' of 1919 and 1920.[101] Kevin O'Shiel, a young barrister, was approached by the 'illegal' Irish government established after the 1918 general election and asked to investigate an outbreak of agrarian violence in the west. A claim published in the *Connacht Tribune* in 1920 that violence was 'sweeping through the west like a prairie fire' may have been overly sensational,[102] but the intensity of agrarian agitation that year is demonstrated by the officially returned 'agrarian outrages', which were higher in 1920 than in any year since 1882, at the height of the Land War.[103] In a series of articles published in the *Irish Times* in 1966, O'Shiel recalled a group of men who marched through Connacht in 1920 branding cattle with the initials 'S.F.' (Sinn Féin) and hanging the tricolour over confiscated land.[104] A number of those participating in the land seizures were farmers who had already obtained land under the land-purchase Acts and wanted to add to their, in some cases, already substantial holdings. Some were poorer tenant farmers who had received land, but as the land given to the poorer farmers tended to be poor land, their circumstances were largely unchanged. Many of those involved had not benefited from these Acts at all and were simply seeking access to farming land for their day-to-day subsistence needs. Thus, O'Shiel referred to the agitators that he encountered as 'the tenants of unviable holdings, who for years were expecting allotments on ...

[grazing] lands'.[105] In the words of Gearóid Ó Tuathaigh, continuing conflict over land after the initial and most renowned land-purchase Acts should be viewed in the context of 'the simple unassuaged ache of land hunger felt by many vulnerable smallholders, who came to realise that the "victory" of the Land War had made little difference to their standard of living'.[106]

In one of the aforementioned *Irish Times* articles, O'Shiel referred to the particularly 'aggressive "Bolshie" spirit' of the agitators he encountered in County Roscommon.[107] Upon his arrival there in 1920 he found that 'most of ... [the] ranches had been cleared of their stock, and roads and lanes, all over the county, were choked with wandering and half-starved beasts'.[108] The Roscommon agitators, he concluded, were 'exceptionally bad'.[109] Even the IRA could not persuade them to rebuild farm walls that they had pulled down.[110] Ó Tuathaigh, a more recent commentator, has outlined why the seizure of land was especially prevalent in that part of Connacht. In County Roscommon, where there were large tracts of untenanted land under the control of the Congested Districts Board, small farmers and landless labourers, Ó Tuathaigh explains, were not simply concerned with the long-term issue of land redistribution; more immediately they required access to conacre land for survival.[111] Thus, as early as 1917, two years before land seizures were occurring on a regular basis in other western counties, estates were invaded in Arigna, Warren, Mockmoyne and Tinnecarra 'by hundreds of small farmers, lightly armed with loys and an occasional pitchfork', the police arriving to find that strips had already been apportioned and 'digging was in full swing'.[112]

These communal land seizures were taking place during the decade we are currently commemorating, posing a challenge to the narrowly defined concept of land ownership that underpinned the land-purchase Acts. However, as the earlier sections of this book might lead us to expect, they have received relatively little scholarly attention when compared to that devoted to the land Acts. As previously stated, the 'proportionality' that the official commemorative process is so keen to protect is based on the distinction found in mainstream history writing between occurrences that are central/significant and occurrences that are peripheral/insignificant. Thus, it is hardly surprising that the land bills are included in the Decade of Centenaries website amongst 'the events that shaped Ireland in the early twentieth century'[113] while the communal land seizures are not mentioned at all. This comparative neglect not only indicates that the aforementioned distinction between that which is central/significant and that which is peripheral/insignificant inevitably favours occurrences and individuals directly associated with the narrowly defined political arena and believed to have had the most impact on what happened afterwards; it is also indicative of the tendency within mainstream history writing to view insurgency that originates from outside of this narrowly defined political arena from the perspective of those seeking to contain it.

Avant-garde Nostalgia

In a now canonical 1944 article, 'The Gaelic Cult', the Cork-born writer and cultural critic Sean O'Faolain condemned Connolly's theorisation of Gaelic communism, categorising Connolly's valorisation of common ownership of land in Gaelic Ireland as a form of nationalist nostalgia. This assessment was shared by a later commentator, Roy Foster; in *The Story of Ireland* Foster referred to James Connolly as 'a Marxist who wanted to turn back the clock to precapitalism believing (a la O'Grady) that ancient Ireland had pioneered communism'.[114] O'Faolain and Foster, in their evaluations of Connolly's Gaelic communism, focused primarily on the backward look, interpreting this concept in the context of the more mainstream strands of an Irish Revival movement that, in their opinion, had foolishly sought to restore an earlier 'lost' world. However, as previously demonstrated here, Connolly's Gaelic communism involved a simultaneous backward/forward look. Moreover, it was propelled by the actions of contemporary poorer rural dwellers. In addition, even if we accept that there was a nostalgic component to Gaelic communism, I would suggest this nostalgia is perhaps most usefully catagorised as an 'avant-garde nostalgia'.[115] In the writings of the British philosopher Kate Soper, avant-garde nostalgia is pitted against both the 'simple backward look' with its patrician and sometimes patriarchal forms of nostalgia and the 'simple progressive thrust' with its unthinking adulation of capitalist progress, the truly progressive lying beyond this antithesis.[116]

What functions were served by the simultaneous backward/forward look in the period leading up to the establishment of the Irish Free State? Avant-garde nostalgia, as utilised at this point in time, clearly had a pragmatic dimension. As Gregory Dobbins points out, while absolute ownership of land was indeed rare in early Irish society, Connolly's depiction of the land system in pre-colonial Ireland was, to some extent, an idealised one designed to 'redirect "the traditional" away from a conventional nationalist project' and create an indigenous precedent for socialism.[117] But radical forms of nostalgia during the decade we are currently commemorating also served to disrupt and counter linear narratives of progress, whether these narratives underpinned imperialism, bourgeois nationalism, capitalism or metropolitan Marxism. Connolly envisaged Gaelic communism neither as a turning back of the clock nor as an uninterrupted movement forwards but as an advanced, forward-thinking form of socialism grounded in that which colonial commentators had viewed as backward practices that inhibit progress. Moreover, in his theorisation of Gaelic communism he resisted the facile normalisation of the present that sustains dominant power structures. While acknowledging that 'the adherent of the present order of society will regard it [clan ownership as it existed in Ireland] as proof of the Irish incapacity for assimilating progressive ideas', he insisted that it should instead be viewed as the bedrock of future alternative social possibilities.[118] For Connolly, therefore, the future lay not in the past per se but in that which had been dismissed in the past as regressive, even barbaric. Thus, Connolly's backward/forward look can be differentiated from bourgeois nationalism, which, though often dependent upon a simultaneous appeal to tradition and modernity, smoothes over 'the potentially liberating jagged edges of the past and make[s] it safe for consumption' as justification for itself.[119] As Gregory Dobbins points out, it was paradoxically this very process of smoothing over the jagged edges of the past that facilitated the muting of Connolly's own radicalism and his absorption into the traditional nationalist canon.[120]

In the period leading up to the establishment of the Free State, avant-garde nostalgia allowed for some of the most radical and utopian imaginings of a future Ireland. Hence, the unrealised yet possible past futures from that point in time which I am most interested in commemorating are those that have their origins (if we can talk about unrealised futures as having origins!) in that which challenged both the 'simple backward look' and the 'simple progressive thrust'. The Irish historian Joe Lee has quite rightly pointed out that 'the "if only" school of history' suffers from 'an abiding temptation ... to assume that the alternative to what really happened would have been an ideal situation',[121] and certainly, if we view each past moment as if its future were potentially multiple as opposed to singular, we must acknowledge that not all of that moment's contingencies are desirable. As is the case with conventional history, the casting of lateral shadows involves a selection process. The roads untaken that, in my view, are best positioned to become the focus of a radical commemoration process are the truly progressive, as defined by Kate Soper: those that were grounded in a concept of change that challenged a linear narrative of progress.

Another example of avant-garde nostalgia of this sort in the decade that we are currently commemorating involved drawing on the Brehon laws when imagining an enhanced role for women in a future independent Ireland. In early modern Ireland the Brehon laws had been dismissed by colonial commentators as 'lewd' or 'barbarous' custom. However, in 1852 the British government, having been instructed that these laws had 'important bearings upon the existing condition of society in Ireland',[122] agreed to fund a project to transcribe, translate, edit and make available for publication the Brehon-law manuscripts. A commission comprised mainly of members of the Anglo-Irish elite was established to oversee the project, and the Gaelic scholars John O'Donovan and Eugene O'Curry commenced work on the law tracts early in 1853. Legal experts, historians and Irish-language experts subsequently wrote introductions to the individual volumes. The result of this translation project, which took almost fifty years to complete, was a six-volume collection titled *The Ancient Laws and Institutes of Ireland*.

Pre-colonial Irish law was constructed for a society that was patrilineal and, therefore, patriarchal. That said, it contained elements that lent themselves to a later feminist alignment with this body of law. This is indicated in some of the scholarly writings that accompanied the Brehon-law translations. For example, in the preface to the second volume of *The Ancient Laws and Institutes of Ireland*, W. Neilson Hancock, a former professor of jurisprudence at Queen's College, Belfast and Thaddeus O'Mahony, professor of Irish at Trinity College, Dublin stated the following:

> At a time when the English law of husband and wife, which has now, for three centuries, been substituted for the Irish law in this country, has been condemned by a Committee of the House of Commons, as unjust towards the wife, and when the most advanced of modern thinkers are trying to devise some plan by which wives may be placed in a position more nearly approaching to equality with the husband, it is interesting to discover in the much despised law of the ancient Irish, the recognition of the principle on which efforts are being made to base our legislation on this subject.[123]

The principle that Hancock and O'Mahony were referring to in this passage can be found in the old Irish tract *Cáin Lánamna* [the Law of Couples] from the law collection titled *Senchus Mór*. The tract, written about 700, includes legislation regarding the rights of a woman who enters a marriage with equal wealth to her husband. A wife, under these circumstances, was recognised as having equal rights in the marriage and only in certain

exceptional circumstances was her husband permitted
to enter into any contract or legal arrangement without
her consent. Hancock and O'Mahony, in their preface,
were contrasting this legislation with English common
law, under which a woman's wealth, unless special
arrangements were put in place, automatically became
her husband's following marriage.[124]

Both contemporaneous and more recent writings
about the Dáil Courts likewise draw attention to the
role played by the Brehon laws in debates concerning
the status of Irish women, in this case in the period
just prior to, and directly after, the establishment of the
Free State. The Dáil Courts of 1920–24 (also known as
the Republican Courts) were an integral component in
what had become, by the early twentieth century, one
of the central strategies of Irish anti-colonial resistance:
the displacement of 'British' political and administrative
institutions by de facto alternatives. These courts have
been aptly described by Mary Kotsonouris as 'extraordinary courts that operated in an ordinary way' in
that, for the most part, they adopted the ethos and value
system of official legal institutions.[125] The Dáil Court
system was comprised of a Supreme Court, a District
Court in every parliamentary constituency, and a local
court in every Roman Catholic parish. Notwithstanding
the overlaps between this legal system and the one it was
seeking to displace, the guidelines drawn up for the use
of Dáil Court judges, published in 1921 and titled *Ju-
diciary*, state that while the law previously in force, the
common law of England, was to be retained, reference

could be made in court to 'the early Irish Law Codes, or any commentary upon them in so far as they may be applicable to modern conditions'.[126] James Creed Meredith, who had held the position of King's Counsel under the official legal system, transferred his loyalties to the Dáil Courts upon their establishment, and was appointed president of its Supreme Court. Interestingly, Meredith, the Dáil Court judge who had most experience of official law, was also one of the strongest exponents of the incorporation of the Brehon laws into the Dáil Courts system. For example, in 1920, while presiding over a case involving a single mother who was seeking monetary support from the father of her child, Meredith, proclaiming common law retrograde in such matters, gave his judgment in accordance with what he referred to as the spirit of the Brehon laws. The woman was awarded a sum of money in compensation for the expenses she had accrued looking after the child in question. Meredith, in an account of this episode published in 1940 in the *Journal of the Statistical and Social Inquiry Society of Ireland*, claimed that this case, which was tried in County Cork, 'was subsequently followed uniformly in the Republican Courts'.[127]

Perhaps not surprisingly, the majority of the women who drew on the Brehon laws when advocating for improved conditions for contemporary Irish women were republicans by politics. Dorothy Macardle, in her book-length account of the Irish War of Independence and its aftermath, wrote in glowing terms of Meredith's adoption of the Brehon laws in cases involving single mothers. Indeed, Macardle stated that, in general, 'an enlightened attitude towards women prevailed' in the Dáil Courts, justifying this claim with reference to the practice of having a woman amongst the judges on the bench when a woman was being tried.[128] Whether or not this practice was as commonplace as Macardle suggests, it is certainly true that women did, at times, preside over Dáil Court hearings. This was in part facilitated by the fact that while the judges of the Supreme Court had to have formal training in the official legal system, no such qualification was deemed necessary for the lower courts. Thus, the vast majority of those who presided over them were laypeople elected by the local Sinn Féin Club. Kathleen Clarke, Maud Gonne MacBride and Hanna Sheehy-Skeffington are amongst the women who availed of the opportunity to preside over Parish Court sittings.[129] As pointed out by David Foxton in *Revolutionary Lawyers*, it took independent Ireland over forty years to come even close to matching this level of involvement of women in the legal system.[130]

Another woman who connected the Brehon laws with a broadly feminist project was the Irish mathematician and educator Sophie Bryant. Bryant's account of old Irish law was written during the decade we are currently commemorating, and published in 1923. The title of Bryant's book, *Liberty, Order and Law Under Native Irish Rule*, might suggest that this is a work of straightforward historical scholarship, but there are strong indications that this is not how Bryant herself viewed the publication. The past, for her, was clearly a resource for those in the present attempting to create a future that was both better than, and different from, that present. Thus, Bryant's book is dedicated to 'the patron saints of Ireland Padraigh and Brigid and to the re-builders of Ireland united and free'.[131] In the preface she states her hope that *Liberty, Order and Law Under Native Irish Rule* would prove to be 'of service' to her 'countrymen and countrywomen in the work of social reorganisation that lies before them'.[132] 'In the work of regeneration for the future that lies before the Irish people', she claims, 'a more widely diffused and accurate knowledge of the old Irish customs should be of great value.'[133] Bryant's book provides a detailed account of such woman-related aspects of the Brehon laws as 'illegitimacy', the status of women within marriage, property laws relating to women, and the right of women to divorce their husbands. The book also suggests that the Brehon laws might assist Bryant's contemporaries in thinking in constructive ways about women and work. In this context Bryant cites from the Brehon-law manuscripts as follows: '"If a woman has the full work of a woman", says the text, "whether it [the work] be productive or non-productive, she shall obtain [the value of] the full work of the man."'[134] In urging those who wished to participate in the regeneration of Ireland's future to increase their knowledge of old Irish customs, Bryant, like Connolly, was engaging in a simultaneous backward/forward look. She was grounding a forward-thinking feminism in that which had previously been dismissed as backward practices.

The Angel of History

Connolly famously died in 1916, one of sixteen men executed by the British authorities for playing a leading role in the Rising. Sophie Bryant, a considerably less well-known figure both during her lifetime and now, died at the end of the decade we are currently commemorating, 1922, the year the Irish Free State was established.[135] It is highly unlikely that either would have heard of the then young Walter Benjamin, whose earliest works were published in the 1920s, yet both Connolly's and Bryant's advocacy of that which had been dismissed as regressive and thus an obstacle to progress calls most compellingly to mind Benjamin's writings, in particular his later ninth thesis on history. Benjamin, a German Jew, killed himself on the French–Spanish border in 1940 at the age of forty-eight in anticipation of being handed over by French collaborationist government officials to the Nazi Gestapo. Shortly before his unsuccessful attempt to flee Vichy France, he wrote one of his last major works. This short essay, 'Theses on the Philosophy of History', is composed of twenty numbered paragraphs that offer a sustained and, at times, highly emotive critique of 'professional' history writing. In it he claimed that to articulate 'the past historically does not mean recognising it "the way it really was"'. Benjamin countered a positivistic historicism that he associated with nineteenth-century scholars, such as Leopold von Ranke, with an historical materialism that seizes hold of 'a memory' that 'threatens both the content of the tradition and those

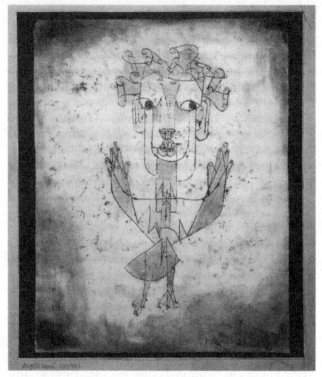

Figure 4: Paul Klee, *Angelus Novus*, 1920. Source: Public Domain –
Wikimedia Commons.

who inherit it'.[136] This memory, which 'flashes up at a
moment of danger', must be forcibly held, as every image of the past that is not recognised by the present
as one of its own concerns threatens to disappear irre-
trievably.[137] Notwithstanding the force of such passages,
it is in his ninth thesis that Benjamin most eloquent-
ly challenged the progressivist model of history that
underpins mainstream history writing:

There is a picture by Klee called *Angelus Novus*. It shows an angel who seems about to move away from something he stares at. His eyes are wide, his mouth is open, his wings are spread. This is how the angel of history must look. His face is turned towards the past. Where a chain of events appear before *us*, *he* sees one single catastrophe, which keeps piling wreckage upon wreckage and hurls it at his feet. The angel would like to stay, awaken the dead, and make whole what has been smashed. But a storm is blowing from Paradise and has got caught in his wings; it is so strong that the angel can no longer close them. This storm drives him irresistibly into the future, to which his back is turned, while the pile of debris before him grows towards the sky. What we call progress is *this* storm.[138]

The past, for Benjamin, was no mere continuum of progress; rather it provides stark evidence of the cataclysmic force of progress. The angel featured in a 1920 Paul Klee ink-wash drawing that Benjamin owned for a time is thus reimagined in this allegory as the Angel of History who looks backward but is forced forward, watching an ever expanding build-up of destruction incessantly accumulate towards the skies. The nature of this destruction is spelt out for us by Benjamin: the debris of progress. While the casualties of the past clearly constitute the bulk of this debris, surely it is at least partially comprised of the many unrealised yet possible past futures that progress has disavowed? But how are we to interpret Benjamin's angel? What can we say about this figure who looks to the past whilst being blown, helplessly open-winged, into the future? Does the angel's inability to stay so that he can 'make whole what has been smashed' speak to and about an ultimately passive relationship to historical loss? Or, as Paul K. Saint-Amour ponders, does the angel's unrelenting temporal gaze urge us to refuse to let such loss be 'chalked up to the cost of progress'?[139] If the latter is the case, as I believe it to be, does Benjamin allow for the emergence of a more dynamic relationship between past, present and future than that initially suggested by the strictly backward gaze of an angel incapable of controlling its movements? Elsewhere in his theses on the philosophy of history, Benjamin stated that 'the chronicler who narrates events without distinguishing between major and minor ones acts in accord with the following truth: nothing that has ever happened should be regarded as lost to history'.[140] This 'nothing' includes the debris of progress. The angel's desire to 'awaken the dead' suggests that this debris can potentially be transformed from that which had been discarded in the past as obsolete to that which is a living force in the present. Indeed, in keeping with Connolly, I would suggest that the debris of progress is a potential resource for a renewal of the present that would allow for a future that is more than the mere extrapolation of present-day power. Included in this resource are the unrealised yet possible past futures that, in the words of Saint-Amour, were 'seen by the past as barred',[141] dormant possibilities that are not lost but simply waiting for us to reactivate them. Thus, brushing history against the grain, as Benjamin famously urged us to do in his seventh thesis on history, reveals a repository of past hopes and preparations for the future that can sustain our current aspirations. In the words of Paul Ricoeur, 'we have so many unfulfilled plans behind us, so many promises that have still not been held, that we have the means of rebuilding the future through reviving our heritage in its multiple forms'.[142]

Returning to our current commemorations, yes, the fast-running conveyor belt of centenaries may at times seem a rather wearisome ordeal. However, I believe that the ten years before the establishment of the Free State was a period potent with possibility, a point in time when the future was most definitely multifarious. What would it take to revive this period in its multiple forms? What would it take to 'remember' the futures that it could potentially have given rise to? It would involve something more and other than bemused and sometimes patronising references to the seemingly odd and eccentric ways of being that were practised or countenanced during the ten-year period we are commemorating.[143] It would involve something more and other than tokenistic gestures towards inclusivity.[144] And it would certainly involve something more and other than offering a balance between nationalist and Revisionist (with a capital 'R') versions of the historical events being commemorated.

Reimagining Commemoration

As can be surmised from my earlier reading of RTÉ's centenary drama *Rebellion*, casting a critical eye over the commemorative events and activities that have taken place as part of Ireland's decade of centenaries thus far is a relatively easy task. It is considerably more difficult and, for the purposes of this book, considerably more important to lay the foundations for alternative forms of commemoration; events and activities that shine a light on the untaken roads of the past. That said, I believe that a useful starting point for such a project is, in fact, our current commemorations. Therefore I will now proceed to take a fresh look at these commemorations. Rather than pick out events and activities to critique, however, I will pinpoint the aspects of the decade of centenaries that overlap with the kinds of critical histories and alternative concepts of historical change that have shaped the writing of this book. In this way I can go beyond mere abstract theorisation, providing actual examples of the kinds of practices and ideas upon which a truly radical commemorative process could be based.

Turning to the hundredth anniversary of the 1916 Rising, the range of events is itself of significance. Some of these were organised by the state, but many, such as the commemorative activities associated with the Women of the South project, were designed and run by groups and individuals not directly connected to the state. The large number of small events that took place throughout the country, particularly south of the border, suggest that Irish people living in the Republic at least feel that they have a stake in the centenaries. Moreover, the holding of a plethora of small events is structurally much more suited than a larger ceremony to the project of reviving the decade we are currently commemorating in its multiple forms. These small events include the ones that made up RTÉ's Reflecting the Rising, the state-associated Easter Monday's multitude of commemorative activities. Reflecting the Rising – comprised of talks, debates, concerts, walking tours, dramatisations, dance, film screenings, exhibitions, and so on – took place in over two hundred locations throughout Dublin city. The structure of that day's commemorations – spread out, decentralised, democratised – ensured that the Easter Monday celebrations were automatically more attuned than the larger Easter Sunday event to that which is at the margins of conventional history writing.

The large numbers of small commemorative events held in 2016 are not the only indicator that Irish people feel that they have a stake in the centenaries. Even the popularity of Rising kitsch – the T-shirts, key rings, calendars, and so on referred to in the opening pages of this book – point to a desire for some form of personal connection to the period in Irish history we are currently commemorating. It would be easy to dismiss these objects en masse and their purchase as yet one more example of inappropriate commodification, the assignment of economic value to something that should not be conceived in economic terms, but surely the urge to own these items is, at least in part, an urge for ownership of the Rising and the interpretation of its meaning? This is perhaps the same urge that compelled so many people to get involved in the campaign to save 16 Moore Street and surrounding houses from demolition. It was to these houses that some of the Rising leaders retreated from the burning GPO in the final hours of the Rising. It is where they met for the last time before their execution. Consequently the Moore Street houses can be considered the last headquarters of the Provisional Government of the Irish Republic. What the popularity of this campaign suggests is that, for many, the Rising and its legacies ultimately belong to Irish people. It was perhaps an awareness of this sense of ownership that prompted the *Irish Times* to publish an article on April Fool's Day 2017 on the purchase of Liberty Hall by a company connected to Donald Trump. The article included details on the transformation of the iconic building into a five-star hotel, bearing Trump's name, with an open-air putting green on the top floor, and cited a very plausible Trump tweet regarding the business deal:

'Bought a small tower in Dublin, Ireland. We are going to build an awesome hotel in Dublin. It will be totally great! Love Ireland! Great country!'[145] The humour of the piece, of course, relies on a general awareness that any attempt to Trumpify that particular 'small tower' would likely result in another Rising. On a more serious note, the notion of the Rising and its legacies belonging to the people of Ireland is also indicated by one of the contemporary uses made of another building connected to the 1916 insurrection: the GPO. It is notable that almost all marches and demonstrations held in Dublin in support of justice and equality, whether linked to domestic or international issues, ultimately converge at the steps of this building. As Clair Wills points out, the GPO is something other than just a post office, though it 'is not a politician's building' and 'not (yet) a museum'.[146] It is a focal point for political protest that allows current injustices to be viewed through the prism of the ideals of the period we are currently commemorating.

Considerable attention is paid in this book to avant-garde nostalgia during the decade we are now commemorating, but avant-garde nostalgia is also a factor in our own time and has helped shape some of the more radical commemorations of that decade. Speaking in Liberty Hall following one of the last state events of Easter weekend, a wreath-laying ceremony at the statue of James Connolly in Beresford Terrace, President Michael D. Higgins stated that 'land and private property, a restrictive religiosity and a repressive pursuit of respectability, affecting women in particular, became the defining social and cultural ideals of the newly independent Ireland'. Moreover, he claimed, the republic for which Connolly and the Irish Citizen Army hoped remained unfulfilled in present-day Ireland,[147] though 'their aspirations could still sustain us today in rebuilding our society and our economy'.[148] However, notwithstanding the important contributions of President Higgins, the most notable example of a commemorative event shaped by present-day avant-garde nostalgia thus far in the decade of centenaries was the 1916 parade, pageant and concert organised by the Reclaim the Vision of 1916 initiative. Scheduled for the calendar centenary of the Rising, the Reclaim the Vision of 1916 commemorations offered a socio-economic and political vision that was grounded, where possible, in the dreams and aspirations that underpinned the 1916 Proclamation. For many of those involved in putting together the Reclaim the Vision commemorations, not only has the vision of the Proclamation not yet been achieved, the dreams and aspirations that inspired it were wholly betrayed in recent years by the Irish men and women who gained most from the Celtic Tiger economic boom and suffered least following its collapse. Thus, in their Proclamation for a New Irish Republic, the Reclaim the Vision of 1916 initiative declared that in a real Irish democracy,

the common good would come before the freedom of capital and the markets or the pursuit of private profit. The wealth of the country belongs to the people, and the natural resources, industries and services

> must be utilised in the interests of all the people and subjected to their democratic control.[149]

This passage, of course, echoes James Connolly's earlier advocacy of the

> democratic principle that property was intended to serve the people, and not by the principle so universally acted upon at present, viz. that the people have no other function in existing than to be the bondslaves of those who by force or by fraud have managed to possess themselves of property.[150]

A key component of the Reclaim the Vision project is its call upon Irish citizens to work toward the Rising's vision of 'a republic of equality and opportunity with nobody marginalised, left behind or forgotten'.[151] The commitment of the initiative to this aspect of the project can be gauged from the active support and involvement in the Reclaim the Vision of 1916 commemorations of organisations such as the Pavee Point Traveller and Roma Centre, which advocate for social justice for those on the margins of Irish society.

Avant-garde nostalgia in the present, just like avant-garde nostalgia in the decade we are commemorating, has the potential to disrupt and counter linear narratives of progress, including the aggressively forward-thrusting rhetoric of change that underpins neoliberalism and that shapes neoliberal subjectivity. Just as some Irish men and women during the decade we are currently commemorating grounded their vision of a future post-independence Ireland in a Gaelic past, those involved in the Reclaim the Vision of 1916 initiative evoked the principles of the 1916 Proclamation when calling for an alternative to a neoliberal Ireland.

Much of this book has been concerned with the potentially liberating jagged edges of the past. However, there are also elements in present-day Irish society that don't always fit smoothly, posing a challenge to the narratives that underpin socio-economic norms. The points at which these elements came up against the 1916 commemoratory celebrations gave rise to some of the more interestingly provocative components of the decade of centenaries thus far. Of particular note was the scheduling of the television programme *I Am Traveller* for 24 March, the Thursday before the principal official 1916 events. The programme itself was not formally part of the commemoration itinerary, but it was connected to that itinerary in that it was part of a documentary series shown on RTÉ that was seeking, in the context of the centenaries, to challenge narrow notions of Irishness. As a whole the three-part series – comprised of *I Am Traveller*, *I Am Immigrant* and *I Am Irish* – made for compelling viewing, rewriting Irishness by highlighting the diverse range of people that comprise the contemporary Irish populace. However, *I Am Traveller* created a particularly insightful friction with 1916 centenary events. As the titles of the three episodes collectively suggest, the focus of the documentary series is identity in today's Ireland, but the Traveller voices and perspectives that it features ensures that *I Am Traveller* goes considerably beyond its original brief. These voices and perspectives are channelled through John Connors, a Traveller man who by virtue of his fame as an actor in the Irish crime drama *Love/Hate* has been forced to become a mouthpiece for Irish Travellers, whether he chooses to be or not.[152] The series as a whole holds up for critical interrogation the set of ideas that are regularly employed, whether overtly or covertly, when establishing the boundaries of Irish identity. However, *I Am Traveller* reveals that it is a more fundamental taken-for-granted understanding of what it is to be human, including perceived notions of how to live and be in the world, that produces the most damaging forms of exclusion, whether in Ireland or elsewhere. This is particularly evident in the case of those, such as Irish Travellers, whose way of life has traditionally been bound up with practices that pose a challenge to the socio-economic structures that these supposed common-sense assumptions support.

As previously outlined in this book, in the late nineteenth century, British commentators, including Anthony Trollope, argued that to interfere with absolute property rights was to 'attempt to alter the laws for governing the world'.[153] Private-property rights may form the cornerstone of the capitalist mode of production, but the success of capitalism relies on the widespread acceptance of such rights as the cornerstone of what it is to be human. The threat to the natural order that Trollope and others believed was posed by Gladstone's land Acts can be equated to the threat that some believe to be posed by the transient lifestyle traditionally associated with Irish Travellers. In its most recent manifestation this perceived threat finds a focal point in the figuring of rural crime as a code for gangs of rootless/ruthless Travellers preying on respectable property-owners.[154]

Referring back to Benjamin's Angel of History, amongst the many insights offered by *I Am Traveller* is the revelation that Travellers' lives – both their actual lives (sometimes shockingly short) and their way of life – have formed a core component of the debris of 'progress' in the Irish context. Perhaps the most poignant of the many poignant scenes that make up this programme is John Connors' exchange with a young man who, despite his own heroic behaviour on the night in question, lost multiple members of his family in a fire at a halting site in Carrickmines on 10 October 2015. Though only fifteen years old at the time, he succeeded in rescuing one of his brother's children from the blaze, but ten people died in the fire, including five other children.[155]

When asked, whilst standing amongst the debris of that site, a well-meaning question about education and the future directions that his life might take, the young man, clearly frustrated by the mismatch between what he is being asked and the story of devastation and death that he has just told, offers a passionate response that indicates just how alienated he feels from conventional narratives of personal development: 'I don't know how your future would be alright. I can't say, yeah, my future's going to be deadly. It's surely not going to be.

To have to think about my brother, to have to think about being in beside him, with the fire extinguishers that wouldn't work. Sure how would you think of your future being good?'[156]

As previously discussed in this book, alternative approaches to land and land usage formed the basis for some of the possible roads that could have been taken in the run-up to the establishment of the Free State. 'Progress' in the Irish context involved the more communal concepts of land and property countenanced by some small tenant farmers, some landless labourers and some individuals like James Connolly in the decade that we are now commemorating being largely supplanted in the post-revolutionary period by an overly rigid and stringently enforced concept of private ownership. This rigid concept of private ownership is grounded in the land-purchase Acts introduced by the British Conservative Party. However, it was sanctified in the post-revolutionary period by a national narrative that mapped the ownership of Ireland by the Irish onto private-property rights by suggesting that the colonial struggle was all about owning the land – taking it back from the landlords – with ownership interpreted here in the narrowest sense of the term. Owner occupation in Free State Ireland, as Seamus Deane has pointed out, 'closed the gap between soil and land', with soil 'as what land [a politico-legal entity] becomes when it is ideologically constructed as a natal source, that element out of which the Irish originate and to which their past generations have returned'.[157] That this national narrative remained prevalent long after the establishment of both the Free State and Republic is signalled by an extract from a report by John Holden published in the *Irish Times* at the height of the Celtic Tiger property bubble: 'The Plantation, Land Wars, and the Famine years are certain to have had an impact on every Irishman wanting his own plot.'[158] This overlapping of the ownership of Ireland by the Irish with the private ownership of property and land has manifested itself in multiple ways since the founding of the state. In the earlier stages of the Free State it allowed for the establishment of a precedent whereby home ownership was to be prioritised over all other housing issues. Thus, in the 1920s, owner-occupancy, supported by government policy and generous subsidies to private builders, was put forward as the best available means for combating all housing-related concerns in Ireland, including the considerable problems posed by the still-prevalent tenements and slums of Dublin, Limerick and Cork.[159] The following passage, published in the *Irish Builder and Engineer*, suggests that the Irish building industry, even in the early years of the Free State, felt itself to be in a particularly advantageous position: 'it was gratifying, in these days of socialism, to find the head of State disassociating himself from the foolish notions that some have, that the whole of such vast [housing] problems have only to be made a government concern to be solved.'[160] While there were public housebuilding programmes at intervals in the period between, it is not difficult to find overlaps between

Cumann na nGaedheal's decision in the mid-1920s 'to reduce the level of construction undertaken by local authorities, and instead divert public funds to private builders (via grants and tax breaks)' and the developer-friendly policy decisions made by later Irish governments that contributed to an over-heated housing market during the Celtic Tiger period.[161]

Notwithstanding the fact that home ownership in Ireland, contrary to popular perception, is in line with other countries in Europe,[162] the mapping of the ownership of Ireland by the Irish onto private-property rights and the subsequent establishment of owner-occupancy as the housing norm have given rise to an especially negative attitude in Ireland towards those over a certain age who rent their homes rather than own them. Living in rented accommodation as an older adult is viewed here as dysfunctional, particularly if the renter in question is not actively seeking to become an owner at some stage in the near future. Thus, even when house prices rise to untenable levels, as with the property bubble from the late 1990s to 2007, the pressure to buy and own property is extreme. Empathy for those in their thirties, forties and older who fail to get on the 'property ladder' and then, due to a rent hike, become homeless is invariably mixed with suspicion: why were they still renting at this stage of their lives? This sus-picion can be tinged with disapproval if those involved have children: why didn't they do the responsible thing and wait until they had bought a house before starting a family?

The repercussions on the Traveller community of the mapping of the ownership of Ireland by the Irish onto private-property rights have been particularly severe. Essentially this national narrative ensured that there has been no physical and conceptual space possible within the official parameters of the post-revolutionary Irish state for those whose way of life was traditionally founded on different practices and principles of land and land usage. In *The Travellers*, a more recent three-part documentary series that also features John Connors, members of the Traveller community make reference to the widely accepted notion amongst non-Travellers that the origins of contemporary Irish Travellers can be traced to the Great Famine. Travellers, according to this origin narrative, are the descendants of impoverished tenant farmers and labourers who were evicted from their homes in the 1840s and '50s, and forced to adopt a transient lifestyle, spending their subsequent lives reluctantly wandering the roads and lanes of Ireland.[163] As pointed out in *The Travellers*, Irish Travellers, in this version of their emergence as a distinct group in Irish society, are broken settled people who require fixing. Moreover, non-Travellers are encouraged via this narrative to conclude that the most suitable form that this fixing could take is reinstatement in a fixed location. In this context Connors alludes to the infamous 1963 *Report of the Commission on Itinerancy*, a key policy document that identified the main 'problem with Travellers' as their lack of fixed abode and the main remedy as a systematic settlement-and-assimilation programme. Given the aforementioned widely accepted origin myth, this document could be viewed by non-Travellers as a benign project that merely seeks to correct the damage of the Famine. However, responding to this document from the perspective of an Irish Traveller, Connors categorises it as an aggressive attack on a way of life associated with the Travelling community, pointing out, in *I Am Traveller*, that it was perhaps no coincidence that the report was put forward as the 'final solution' to the Traveller 'problem'.

A commemoration process that celebrates the possibilities offered by the more radical and/or utopian ways of imagining Ireland in the run-up to, and shortly after, the establishment of the Free State would allow us to conjure up the history of a post-revolutionary Ireland that might have been. While these unrealised past futures clearly can't solve all of our current problems, commemoration of this sort could nonetheless provide a rich resource for reimagining Ireland today. Those of us who want to imagine a future Ireland very different from the current one – an Ireland in which everyone can believe that she/he has a future – have much to gain by thinking with those who lived during the decade we are now commemorating about the worlds they envisaged, notwithstanding the fact that the realisation of these worlds was foreclosed by the post-revolutionary Irish state.

Arguably, the current political climate in Ireland is potentially fertile ground for such a commemoration process. The election that took place on the centenary of 1916 and the response to that election suggest a tentative end to the Civil War political divide between

Fine Gael and Fianna Fáil. Given that Fianna Fáil's sentimental attachment to the concept of a united Ireland has historically had as little impact on partition as Fine Gael's long-standing policy of non-intervention in Northern affairs, this reshaping of the Irish political landscape seems long overdue. Could the ending of this relatively bogus political divide allow for the emergence of a new form of political alignment grounded in concepts of justice and equality, including economic equality? I should point out that I am not as gung-ho about this election as Fintan O'Toole, who, by focusing on Fianna Fáil's rhetoric of fairness in the run-up to the election, interpreted even the increased vote for this party as signalling a rejection of the neoliberal agenda.[164] However, I do believe that in 2016 we witnessed an at least partial rejection by the Irish electorate of a mindset that prioritises the economy, narrowly defined as the market, over all else.

As previously stated in this book, periods of potent possibility are characterised by a prevailing belief – often connected to the collapse of dominant socio-political formations or ideologies – that the future can be very different from the present and that it can be shaped by those living in that present.[165] Are we therefore currently living through a period that is itself particularly potent with possibility? I believe this to be the case. As previously asserted, periods of potent possibility can generate a greater number of fictional works that contain counterfactual elements. Is the period we are now living through, like the decade we are currently commemorating, giving rise to a greater than normal number of literary works of this kind? Are Kevin Barry's *Beatlebone* (2015), centred on a 1978 trip that John Lennon did not make to Clew Bay, and Mary Morrissey's structurally counter-factual *Prosperity Drive* (2016), a text that clearly finds inspiration in Joyce's *Dubliners*, precursors to a new counterfactual phase in Irish literature? The 2016 Irish election, notwithstanding the formation of the current government, suggests that there are multiple roads that could be taken.[166] It suggests that the future is far from certain. It suggests that the future is, in fact, multifar-ious. Indeed, the idea of 'the Republic' itself seems be up for grabs in a way that it perhaps hasn't been since Irish independence. In the opening pages of this book I reminded the reader that we, in Ireland, are currently living through a decade of centenaries marking a chain of events in Irish history that commenced with the in-troduction of the Third Home Rule Bill and concluded with the establishment of the Irish Free State. However, that may not be the fullest and most accurate descrip-tion of the present moment. What we are living through is not simply a decade of centenaries but an interest-ing conflation of periods of time, our current period of possibility overlapping with the commemoration of another period of possibility. As Tina O'Toole has quite rightly pointed out, this is a very different scenario than if the decade of centenaries had fallen during the Celtic Tiger period, a time marked by 'national triumphalism' and 'neolibeal individualism'.[167] In the current, far less certain political and economic climate, a commemoration process that does not seek to petrify the past, but instead acknowledges that the past could have been other than it was and that it could have given rise to other possible futures, could assist us in the difficult but necessary process of imagining our future as other/better than the here and now.

In conclusion, I am calling for a radical rethinking of commemoration in the context of Ireland's decade of centenaries. Given that we are already at the decade's mid point, this intervention is a timely one. The commemoration process that I am advocating is one that is informed by critical histories. What kinds of occurrences would be remembered in a radical commemoration process informed by such histories and what would this remembering entail? Such a commemoration process would involve marking occurrences invariably viewed as marginal, contingent or paradoxical in state-centred history writing. It would remember occurrences that seem out of kilter with their time. It would reveal that the reason why such occurrences do not seem to fit with their time period is that they are not easily subsumed into a seamlessly progressive model of history fixated on the past that resulted in our present. Thus, when viewed from a vantage point shaped by current dominant ideologies, such occurrences appear to lead nowhere. This appearance of leading nowhere in itself indicates that these occurrences may have provided the foundations for other roads: alternative past futures. I am calling for a radical commemoration process that accepts that these divergent roads were not destined to end up as cul-de-sacs, but instead acknowledges that the futures they pointed to could have been possible even if they never came to pass. I am calling for a radical commemoration process that attempts to map out these divergent roads and that speculates on the futures to which they may have led.

Within the university this mapping project would entail a transdisciplinary approach of the type that shapes this book, drawing on a range of materials, including sources traditionally used by historians, cultural scholars, political scientists, sociologists, geographers, anthropologists and folklorists. Transcending disciplinary divisions has the potential to produce what Catherine Chaput refers to in *Inside the Teaching Machine* as 'guerrilla knowledge'. Such knowledge, according to Chaput, 'does not exist in any department but on the margins of every discipline, haunting them all' and 'at the edges of legitimate professional work'.[168] As Chaput points out, the university, for the most part, 'reproduces the boundaries of production, consumption, and regulation that allow capitalism to thrive'. Guerrilla knowledge, by contrast, creates opportunities to conceive of a world outside the 'parameters of capitalism'.[169] To maximise on such opportunities, a radical commemoration process would need to facilitate alliance-building. In the case of university-based scholars, alliance-building would involve a rejection of professional containment, with academics engaging with individuals and movements from outside the university and participating in non-academic dialogues and engagements of all kinds, whether public debates, public meetings, community art projects, workshops or direct action.

But what are good examples of marginal, contingent or paradoxical occurrences in the Irish context, occurrences that seem to be out of kilter with their time and lead nowhere, and which, therefore, could be the focus of a radical commemoration process? Moreover, what would a radical commemoration of these occurrences entail in the context of Ireland's decade of centenaries? Given that land is a recurring trope in this book, I will focus on land-related occurrences, though the ideas that I explore here could be applied more broadly. Gearóid Ó Tuathaigh has argued that the ultimate outcome of the land agitation, 'the most effective socio-political movement of collective action in modern Irish history', was 'the entrenchment of a decidedly individualist system of farm ownership' of the sort that is the norm in contemporary Ireland.[170] Consequently, while he provides examples of other concepts and practices of land usage in nineteenth- and early twentieth-century Ireland, such as land nationalisation and collectivised agriculture, he ultimately dismisses these concepts and practices as 'historical curiosities' and 'non-starter[s]'.[171] Such 'non-starters' could be the focus of a series of radical commemorative events held in 2020, the centenary of heightened agrarian agitation in 1920. As previously pointed out in this book, the officially returned 'agrarian outrages' were higher in 1920 than in any year since the Land War. Some of those involved, particularly in the east of the country, were agricultural labourers seeking better working conditions and wages. In addition to holding strikes, labourers disrupted fairs and attacked farms. Sometimes, as in the case of the 'battle of Fenor' in County Waterford, agitation intensified to the point of open warfare. In this particular case, labourers agitating for an increased harvest bonus were locked out by local farmers, who then attempted to bring in machinery to thresh the corn. In November 1919 some 300 labourers confronted 121 policemen, who were escorting a threshing machine to an anti-union farm. According to the *Munster Express*, 'a pitched battle was fought on the roadside between the police and farm labourers, in which revolver shots, batons, and bayonets, were freely used'.[172] Before the farmworkers dispersed, they 'destroyed 80 tons of hay, over 400 barrels of barley and a large barn'.[173]

But the dominant form that agrarian 'outrages' took at this point in time, particularly in the west, was the seizure of land, often carried out by large groups of men, women and children. Indeed, hundreds of large estates and grazing farms were forcibly taken during this period. In most cases the land was then broken up into tillage holdings for individual small farmers or landless labourers. However, in County Galway, the Creggs Land Committee established a collective farm comprised of thousands of acres of seized land,[174] while the tenants of the absentee landlord James Dennison Going declared a soviet when they took over his 300-acre estate in County Limerick.[175] As Fergus Campbell asserts in *Land and Revolution*, the redistribution of land that resulted from these land seizures posed a challenge to agrarian capitalism and private property rights, as did attempts to establish collective farms.[176] Consequently, for Campbell the outcome of the contest 'between radical and conservative elements ... was not clear at the high point of revolution in 1920–21'.[177] As previously stated, 'proportionality' in the case of both mainstream history writing and mainstream commemoration is based on a distinction between that which is central/significant and that which is peripheral/insignificant. This 'proportionality' ensures that the land bills are included in the Decade of Centenaries website amongst the key events that shaped modern Ireland, while the communal land seizures are not. Thus, 'proportionality' results in a marking of the strengthening of absolute property rights in Ireland under the guise of commemorating 'the transfer of land to those who farmed it',[178] and a sidelining of challenges to agrarian capitalism and the primacy of private property.

Brushing history against the grain, the commemorative events held on the centenary of heightened agrarian agitation in 1920 could remember alternative concepts and practices of land usage in nineteenth- and early twentieth-century Ireland. These would range from the Owenite agrarian communities established by William Thompson and John Scott Vandeleur in pre-Famine Ireland, to tenant farmers' assertions of rights of occupancy and their resistance to farming practices associated with agrarian capitalism, such as grazing. With reference to the period between the commencement of the Land War and the establishment of the Free

State, these events could pay tribute to the concept of land nationalisation as advocated by Michael Davitt, and of Gaelic communism as associated with James Connolly. In its marking of acts of agrarian agitation, including the 1920 land seizures, the commemoration could draw on both British 'history from below' and Indian subalternist history writing, encouraging those partaking in the commemorative events to read these acts in their own terms rather than from the perspective of those who were seeking to contain them.[179] A radical commemoration of Irish agrarian agitation entails reading against the grain the official historical sources, such as archival materials, championed by mainstream historians as the best source for 'what actually happened', combined with an engagement with non-official sources, such as the recollections documented in the National Folklore Collection at University College, Dublin.

What kinds of alliances could be formed in the context of a commemoration of this sort? Speaking from the perspective of someone who works in a university, which individuals and movements from outside the university could university-based scholars engage with? Such a commemoration could be organised in conjunction with individuals and movements in Ireland and elsewhere who currently adhere to, and attempt to advance, an alternative relationship with land and property. This could include the Home Sweet Home coalition and Irish Housing Network, which famously took over the NAMA-owned Apollo House office block on Tara Street in Dublin in December 2016 to provide emergency accommodation for people who were homeless and would otherwise have found it difficult to get shelter over the Christmas period. Amongst those involved in the Home Sweet Home coalition at the time were trade unionists, charity workers and some high-profile individuals such as the aforementioned actor and Traveller activist John Connors. What the occupation of the vacant Apollo House revealed is that the taking over of even empty and derelict buildings is viewed as a threat by landlords and developers, and as a breach of 'the market'. At one stage, the coalition received a solicitor's letter seeking an urgent meeting 'with a view to agreeing an immediate and orderly vacation of the property in the interests of the health and safety of those who are unlawfully trespassing on the property'.[180] I would suggest, however, that the interests being protected were not those of the inhabitants of Apollo House but the interests of individuals whose wealth is largely reliant on the primacy of private property. In occupying Apollo House, the Home Sweet Home activists were asserting an alternative set of rights that they believed surpassed private-property rights, including the rights to dignity and shelter. While acknowledging that homelessness is sometimes the result of a complex set of factors, they drew attention to the incongruity of there being 282 vacant or derelict sites totalling sixty-one hectares of land in central Dublin in the midst of an unprecedented homeless crisis in the city.[181]

Its proximity to Christmas, combined with the involvement of celebrities and high-profile trade-union

activists, ensured that the Home Sweet Home occupation was heavily and, for the most part, positively
reported in the mainstream media. Indeed, one of the
better-known members of the coalition, Oscar-win-
ning singer-songwriter Glen Hansard, was invited onto
RTÉ's premier chat show, *The Late Late Show*, in the week
before Christmas to talk to a mostly receptive audience
about the occupation and the extent to which it consti-
tuted a justifiable act of civil disobedience. Amongst the
less well-known and less well-received Irish movements
that could take part in commemorative events celebrat-
ing alternative concepts and practices of land usage in
Ireland are the former inhabitants of Squat City. Though
it didn't garner nearly as much media attention, Squat
City in Grangegorman, Dublin was a more long-term
initiative, being intermittently home to dozens of squat-
ters from 2013 to 2016. Some squatted there out of
necessity, while others chose to live there, viewing
squatting simultaneously as a political act and a way of
life. To claim the right to occupy an empty premises for
the purpose of living is to challenge a counterintuitive societal norm whereby vacant land and property cannot be
used by those who need it because it is owned by someone who currently has no use for it.

By drawing attention to such side-branching roads
from both the past and the present, the commemorative events held on the centenary of heightened agrarian agitation in 1920 could encourage speculation on a
future alternative relationship with land and property, a
relationship grounded in concepts and practices of use

and occupancy. Another world is indeed possible, a fairer world no longer willing to accept that past and present casualties are an inevitable consequence of change, and no longer willing to believe that the only form change can take is an unrelenting forward thrust. However, notwithstanding a recent global economic crisis and an ongoing environmental one – both of which raise significant questions as to the continuing viability of the world as we know it – the fact that another world is possible is not always evident to us. Shockingly, the end of the world, as suggested by Frederic Jameson, is easier for most people to imagine than the end of capitalism.[182] This stymieing of social imagination is in itself a key obstacle to the emergence of a new, different model of society and a key contributing factor in the widespread acceptance of the current neoliberal world order as simply the way things are. The concept of utopia urgently needs to be reclaimed from being a 'nonexisting locus' to once more being the realm of the 'not yet'.[183] For another world to be possible, we need to know that it is possible. And it is possible – indeed, we can get glimpses of this other world. All we need to do is turn our eyes away from the path of progress and look to the futures towards which certain side-branching roads lead.

Notes and References

1. Liberty Hall is an extremely apt venue for a commemorative activity of this sort. The original Liberty Hall, on the same site, was closely connected to the Rising in that it was the base of the Irish Citizen Army, a force initially established to defend striking Workers. It was also where the Proclamation was first printed, in the basement of the building. Moreover this is not the first time that Liberty Hall has been draped in a banner; following the outbreak of the First World War, a banner proclaiming 'We Serve Neither King nor Kaiser, But Ireland' was hung on the front wall of the original building.

2. Only one of the ten plays included in the programme was written by a woman, and only three of the ten were directed by women. This lack of female representation gave rise to a Waking the Feminists campaign that arguably has had more of an impact on Irish society than the Abbey's scheduled events.

3. Dublin: One City One Book is a Dublin City Council initiative, led by Dublin City Public Libraries. Launched in 2006, it encourages Dubliners to read a selected book connected with Ireland's capital city during the month of April every year. Clearly, this project helps create a canon of Dublin-centric texts. While the Dublin: One City One Book canon includes both well-established classics and newer works, it is notable that of the twelve books chosen since the project's inception, *Fallen* is the only female-authored one.

4. As a 'star' broadcaster on RTÉ, Duffy was afforded multiple opportunities on both radio and television to commemorate the

children injured or killed during the Rising, thereby garnering much publicity for *Children of the Rising*.

5. Ged Martin, *Past Futures: The Impossible Necessity of History* (Toronto: University of Toronto Press, 2004), p. 13.

6. 'Welcome to the Decade of Centenaries Website', p. 2, http://www.decadeofcentenaries.com/ (accessed 30 November 2016).

7. Decade of Centenaries Programme', p. 1, http://www.decadeofcentenaries.com/about/ (accessed 30 November 2016).

8. 'Initial Statement by Advisory Group on Centenary Commemorations', p. 5, http://www.decadeofcentenaries.com/initial-statement-by-advisory-group-on-centenary-commemorations/ (accessed 30 November 2016).

9. David Fitzpatrick, 'Historians and the Commemoration of Irish Conflicts, 1912–23', in John Horne and Edward Madigan (eds), *Towards Commemoration: Ireland in War and Revolution, 1912–23* (Dublin: Royal Irish Academy, 2013), pp. 126–33, p. 126. See also Fitzpatrick's earlier negative assessment of commemoration, particularly as it operates in the Irish context, in 'Commemoration in the Irish Free State: A Chronicle of Embarrassment', in Ian McBride (ed.), *History and Memory in Modern Ireland* (Cambridge: Cambridge University Press, 2001), pp. 184–203.

10. Fitzpatrick, 'Historians and the Commemoration of Irish Conflicts, 1912–23', p. 126.

11. Ibid. pp. 126, 132.

12. Ibid. p. 126.

13. For an overview and analysis of alternative concepts and practices of legality in nineteenth- and early twentieth-century Ireland, see Heather Laird, *Subversive Law in Ireland, 1879–1920: From 'Unwritten Law' to the Dáil Courts* (Dublin: Four Courts Press, 2005).

14. Associated in its earliest manifestations with such figures as Eric Hobsbawm and E.P. Thompson, 'history from below' is

a Marxist-inflected social history that primarily focuses on the peasantry and the urban working class. See Eric Hobsbawm, *Primitive Rebels: Studies in Archaic Forms of Social Movement in the Nineteenth and Twentieth Centuries* (Manchester: Manchester University Press, 1959), and E.P. Thompson, *The Making of the English Working Class* (London: Victor Gollancz, 1963).

15. From the 1980s onwards, the Subaltern Studies Collective has offered a sustained analysis of the role of the subaltern or non-elite colonised subject. Ranajit Guha, the founder member of the group, famously called for the subaltern to be reinterpreted as the 'subject of his own history'. This reinterpretation requires a radical decentring of familiar notions of power, and the political as the subaltern can only be viewed as an historical and political agent if the political arena is extended outside the structures of the state. Ranajit Guha, *Elementary Aspects of Peasant Insurgency in Colonial India* (Delhi: Oxford University Press, 1983), p. 4.

16. Martin, *Past Futures*, p. 13.

17. 'Welcome to the Decade of Centenaries Website', p. 2.

18. Gerda Lerner, *The Majority Finds its Past: Placing Women in History* (Oxford: Oxford University Press, 1979), pp. xiv, 145. See also Mary Cullen, 'Foreword', in Margaret Kelleher and James H. Murphy (eds), *Gender Perspectives in Nineteenth-century Ireland: Public and Private Spheres* (Dublin: Irish Academic Press, 1997), pp. 5–8, p. 5.

19. Indeed, according to Mary E. Daly and Margaret O'Callaghan, a key feature of the 1966 commemoration was 'the relatively low prominence given to women. Cumann na mBan received, at best, marginal attention; the contribution made by women was largely ignored, except for the case of Constance Markievicz, despite the fact that women provided some of the most compelling eye witness accounts of the Rising on Telefís Éireann.' 'Introduction: Irish Modernity and "The Patriot Dead" in 1966', in Mary E. Daly and Margaret O'Callaghan (eds), *1916 in 1966: Commemorating the Easter Rising* (Dublin: Royal Irish Academy, 2007), pp. 1–17, p. 12.

20. Women did indeed play a crucial role in the Rising. Some of those who took part in it were involved in a medical capacity, treating the wounded and tending to the dying. Others were couriers, or were responsible for procuring rations or intelligence. Some transferred arms to seized buildings. For many, such as those who prepared food, their involvement was an extension of their domestic role. However, a minority – including Margaret Skinnider and, more famously, Constance Markievicz – were actively involved in armed conflict. Of late, considerable attention has been paid to a female nurse named Elizabeth O'Farrell, who, on 29 April 1916, delivered the initial surrender to the British military. For some, the airbrushing of O'Farrell out of a press photograph taken at the moment of the official surrender has come to symbolise the airbrushing of women out of this period of Irish history more generally. See, for example, Róisín Higgins, *Transforming 1916: Meaning, Memory and the Fiftieth Anniversary of the Easter Rising* (Cork: Cork University Press, 2012), p. 19.

21. Podcast: Matt Cooper talks to Colin Teevan, *The Last Word*, Today FM, 4 January 2016.

22. See Ronan McGreevy, '*Rebellion* Creator Celebrates Role of Women in the Rising', *Irish Times*, 9 January 2016.

23. Podcast: Matt Cooper talks to Colin Teevan, *The Last Word*, Today FM, 4 January 2016. This is a relatively common feature of historical drama. While generally centred on historical events considered key in mainstream history writing, historical drama often foregrounds fictional characters who, if they had existed, would not have found a place in the history books. These characters may be important focal points for the audience, but, in the logic of the historical frameworks reinforced by the more mainstream versions of this form of drama, they are mere bit players who have been swept up in historical events. This is the case with both *Dr Zhivago*, set in Russia in the first half of the twentieth century, and *Strumpet City*, which tells the stories of 'ordinary' inhabitants of Dublin during the Lockout of 1913.

24. See 'Why Were the 1916 Leaders Cast as Background Characters in *Rebellion*? The Drama's Writer Explains', *The Journal*, 4 January 2016.

25. *RTÉ Guide*, 8 April 1966, p. 6.

26. The BBC had previously employed this format in *Culloden*, a 1964 docudrama about the 1746 Battle of Culloden that was written and directed by Peter Watkins.

27. See Clair Wills, *Dublin 1916: The Siege of the GPO* (London: Profile Books, 2009), p. 208.

28. *Insurrection*, episode 1. The 'startling events off the Kerry coast' referred to in the opening episode of *Insurrection* are the discovery of guns and ammunition on Banna Strand and the subsequent arrest of Roger Casement.

29. For a more critical assessment of Lemass and Whitaker's contribution to the Irish economy, see Conor McCarthy, 'Introduction', *Modernisation: Crisis and Culture in Ireland, 1969–1992* (Dublin: Four Courts Press, 2000), pp. 11– 44. See also Conor McCabe, *Sins of the Father: The Decisions that Shaped the Irish Economy*, revised edition (Dublin: The History Press Ireland, 2013), pp. 61–2, 104–5. For example, McCarthy quite rightly claims that 'the Lemass/Whitaker process effectively passed control of the modernisation of the economy and society of the Republic over to multinational capital. The future role for the business and bureaucratic élite of the Republic would be negotiating markets and financial assistance with the European Economic Community, and facilitating, by means of financial and other incentives, the penetration of the economy by multinationals' (McCarthy, *Modernisation*, p. 31).

30. This quotation is taken from a speech that Lemass made at a dinner to mark the retirement of the Fianna Fáil TD P.J. Burke in October 1965. NAI DT, 97/6/159, 'Rising Commemorations', 9 October 1965.

31. Podcast: Matt Cooper talks to Colin Teevan, *The Last Word*, Today FM, 4 January 2016.

32. Walter Benjamin, 'On the Concept of History', in Howard Eiland and Michael W. Jennings (eds), *Walter Benjamin: Selected Writings*, vol. 4 (Cambridge MA: Belknap Press of Harvard University Press, 2006), pp. 389–400, p. 397.

33. Cited in Roy Foster, *The Story of Ireland* (Oxford: Oxford University Press, 1995), pp. 21–2.

34. James Joyce, *Ulysses* [1922] (Harmondsworth: Penguin, 1972), p. 31.

35. Paul K. Saint-Amour, *Tense Future: Modernism, Total War, Encyclopedic Form* (Oxford: Oxford University Press, 2015), pp. 23, 264.

36. Joyce, *Ulysses*, p. 31.

37. See, for example, comments made by contributors to the Notre Dame-produced three-part documentary series, *1916*, narrated by Liam Neeson.

38. W.B. Yeats, 'Easter 1916', *Selected Poems* (London: Phoenix, 2002), pp. 56–8.

39. Wills, *Dublin 1916*, p. 120.

40. See, for example, the context in which Róisín Higgins cites this passage in *Transforming 1916*, p. 7.

41. Cited in Colin Reid, *The Lost Ireland of Stephen Gwynn: Irish Constitutional Nationalism and Cultural Politics, 1864–1950* (Manchester: Manchester University Press, 2011), p. 9.

42. Cited in Roy Foster, *Vivid Faces: The Revolutionary Generation in Ireland, 1890–1923* (London: Allen Lane, 2014), p. 172.

43. Cited in ibid., p. 6.

44. Early productions of this play sequence in 1922 and 1923 took twelve hours over three days and lost considerable sums of money. Thus, Shaw was probably correct in his assessment of the performability of *Back to Methuselah*.

45. George Bernard Shaw, *Back to Methuselah: A Metabiological Pentateuch* [1921] (Harmondsworth: Penguin, 1977), part iv, act ii, p. 232.

46. Ibid. Falstaff is a well-known fictional figure, a sensual cowardly knight who is assigned a comic role in a number of Shakespearean plays, most notably *Henry IV, Part I* and *Part 2*, in which he is a companion to Prince Hal, the future Henry V.

47. Shaw, *Back to Methuselah*, part iv, act i, p. 190.

48. Ibid. part i, act i, p. 69.

49. Ibid. p. 68.

50. Ibid. part i, act ii, pp. 90, 91.

51. Ibid. part iv, act ii, p. 227.

52. However, it should be acknowledged that aspects of the superhuman world that Shaw creates in this self-proclaimed exposition of creative evolution could, with good reason, be categorised as dystopian rather than utopian. Indeed, it is very likely that the neglect of *Back to Methuselah* in recent times, both in the theatre and in scholarly writings, is attributable not only to the difficulties involved in performing this work but to some of its content. For example, eugenics and sanctioned euthanasia would appear to be key elements in the creation of Shaw's race of 'normal' people who live to the age of three hundred and beyond. Ibid. part iv, act i, p. 194.

53. Ibid. part i, act i, p. 67. *Back to Methuselah* is not the only work by Shaw that contains counterfactual elements. The 1912 preface to Shaw's *John Bull's Other Island* is also relevant here. This preface is amongst a number of speculative writings inspired by the Third Home Rule Bill that provide a vision of Ireland under Home Rule. In this preface, Shaw suggested that Ulster unionists could be a key component in a new Home Rule regime. Moreover, he hypothesised that Home Rule would 'liberate' Irish Catholics from Catholicism; in Home Rule Ireland, he proclaimed, opposition to the Catholic Church would no longer be viewed as 'treacherously taking the side of England against

... [one's] own country'. George Bernard Shaw, 'Preface', *John Bull's Other Island* [1904] (Harmondsworth: Penguin, 1984), pp. 53–61, p. 56.

54. Juan F. Elices, 'Uchronian Scenarios in the Context of Irish Literature: The Case of C.B. Gilford's *The Crooked Shamrock*', *Estudios Irelandeses*, no. 9 (2014), pp. 35–43, p. 36.

55. Shaw, *Back to Methuselah*, part ii, p. 95.

56. Ibid. part iii, p. 162. As indicated in footnote 50, this future contains elements that few present-day readers would consider either desirable or acceptable.

57. Saint-Amour, *Tense Future*, p. 266.

58. Michael André Bernstein, *Foregone Conclusions: Against Apocalyptic History* (Berkeley CA: University of California Press, 1994), p. 109.

59. In *Foregone Conclusions*, Michael André Bernstein questions whether Robert Musil's *The Man Without Qualities* can be considered 'fully committed' to the casting of lateral shadows given that its protagonist's experiences dominate the text. Bernstein goes on to claim that side-shadowing can be 'best enacted' in 'works like Joyce's *Dubliners* ... in which a whole city or historical era are the real "main characters"' (Bernstein, *Foregone Conclusions*, pp. 109–10).

60. Joyce, *Ulysses*, p. 221.

61. Leopold von Ranke, *Geschichten der Romanischen und Germanischen Völker von 1494–1514*, in Willy Andreas (ed.), *Fürsten und Völker* (Wiesbaden: E. Vollmer, 1957), p. 4. Cited in Leonard Krieger, *Ranke: The Meaning of History* (Chicago: University of Chicago Press, 1977), p. 4.

62. Joep Leerssen, 'Monument and Trauma: Varieties of Remembrance', in Ian McBride (ed.), *History and Memory in Modern Ireland* (Cambridge: Cambridge University Press, 2001), pp. 204–22, p. 209, footnote 6.

63. Ranke, *Geschichten*, p. 4, cited in Krieger, *Ranke*, p. 5.

64. David Scott, *Conscripts of Modernity: The Tragedy of Colonial Enlightenment* (Durham: Duke University Press, 2004), p. 39.

65. Benjamin, 'On the Concept of History', p. 391.

66. Gearóid Ó Tuathaigh, 'Irish Land Questions in the State of the Union', in Fergus Campbell and Tony Varley (eds), *Land Questions in Modern Ireland* (Manchester: Manchester University Press, 2013), pp. 3–24, p. 12. For an overview of the numerical decline of the Irish farm workers, see David Fitzpatrick, 'The Disappearance of the Irish Agricultural Labourer, 1841–1912', *Irish Economic and Social History*, vol. 7 (1980), pp. 66–92.

67. Ibid.

68. See David Lloyd, 'The Subaltern in Motion: Subalternity, the Popular and Irish Working Class History', *Postcolonial Studies*, vol. 8, no. 4 (2006), pp. 421–37, pp. 431–3.

69. Ó Tuathaigh, 'Irish Land Questions in the State of the Union', p. 13.

70. Ibid. In some of his writings, most notably his 1929 novel *Adrigoole*, Peadar O'Donnell, a republican socialist and son of a seasonal migrant worker, sought to document the harsh realities of the life of the migrant agricultural labourer in early twentieth-century Ireland. Patrick MacGill, a former migrant agricultural labourer turned novelist, drew on his personal experiences as an Irish potato gatherer in Scotland in such writings as *Children of the Dead End* (1914) and *The Rat Pit* (1915). It should be pointed out that both O'Donnell and MacGill were born in County Donegal, from which there was an annual summer migration of farm labourers, or 'tatie hokers', to Scotland for potato picking.

71. Benjamin, 'On the Concept of History', p. 391.

72. Ibid., p. 392.

73. Ibid.

74. Saint-Amour, *Tense Future*, p. 21. Whig history is progressivist in that it presents the past as a road that inevitably culminates in liberal democracy and constitutional monarchy.

75. Gregory Dobbins, 'Whenever Green is Red: James Connolly and Postcolonial Theory', *Nepantla: Views from the South*, vol. 1, no. 3 (2000), pp. 605–48, p. 612.

76. Ibid., p. 611.

77. Ibid.

78. In 2003 Lloyd contributed an essay on James Connolly to an *Interventions* special issue on 'Ireland's Modernities' in which he drew comparisons between Connolly's writings and later publications by such key 'national Marxist' thinkers as Frantz Fanon, Amílcar Cabral and José Carlos Mariátegui. Lloyd, 'Rethinking National Marxism: James Connolly and "Celtic Communism"', *Interventions: International Journal of Postcolonial Studies*, vol. 5, no. 3 (2003), pp. 345–70. This was followed, in 2008, by an *Interventions* special issue on Connolly in which Gregory Dobbins refers to him as an anti-colonial revolutionary who was also 'perhaps the first theorist to rethink Marxism according to the specificity of colonial history'. Gregory Dobbins, 'Connolly, the Archive, and Method', *Interventions: International Journal of Postcolonial Studies*, vol. 10, no. 1 (2008), pp. 48–66, p. 48. In 2016 Edinburgh University Press published Conor McCarthy's edited collection *The Revolutionary and Anti-imperial Writings of James Connolly, 1893–1916*, in which McCarthy argues that Connolly's writings are as pertinent to the post-colonial world today as they were to the world that he inhabited.

79. James Connolly, 'Erin's Hope: The End and the Means' (1897), in Donal Nevin (ed.), *Writings of James Connolly*, vol. 2 (Dublin: SIPTU, 2011), pp. 1–22, p. 8.

80. Ibid., p. 3–4.

81. Ibid., p. 2.

82. Ibid.

83. Some passages of this section of the book were published, in an earlier version, in Heather Laird, *Subversive Law in Ireland: From 'Unwritten Law' to the Dáil Courts* (Dublin: Four Courts

Press, 2005). I am grateful to Four Courts Press for permission to include this material here.

84. Though often dismissed in mainstream history writing as little more than an interesting oddity of the Land War period, land nationalisation, as espoused by Davitt, received significant support from sectors within the land movement and the poorer members of the rural community, particularly agricultural labourers. While never officially endorsed by the Land League, it was accepted by central figures within the league, such as John Ferguson, Thomas Brennan, Rev. Harold Rylett and by the newspapers, *Irish World*, *Brotherhood* and the *Belfast Weekly Star* as the most appropriate solution to the Irish land question. Moreover, following the collapse of his political career, Charles Stuart Parnell, perhaps opportunistically, began to campaign for land nationalisation.

85. Michael Davitt, *The Fall of Feudalism in Ireland, or the Story of the Land League Revolution* (London: Harper & Brothers, 1904), p. 94.

86. Ibid., p. 161.

87. Ibid., p. 199.

88. Ibid., p. 161. See John Stuart Mill, *England and Ireland* (London: Longmans, Green, Reader and Dyer, 1868), p. 12.

89. Donal J. O'Sullivan, *The Irish Constabularies, 1822–1922: A Century of Policing in Ireland* (Dingle, Co. Kerry: Brandon, 1999), p. 157.

90. 'An Extraordinary Affair', *Freeman's Journal*, 28 November 1881.

91. 'An Extraordinary Affair', *Freeman's Journal*, 6 December 1881.

92. Shaw, *Back to Methuselah*, part iv, act i, p. 194.

93. For an account of the negative reaction to the 1881 land Act from within Gladstone's cabinet, see Clive Dewey, 'Celtic Agrarian Legislation and the Celtic Revival: Historicist

Implications of Gladstone's Irish and Scottish Land Acts, 1870–1886', *Past & Present*, no. 64 (1974), pp. 30–70, p. 59.

94. Philip Bull, *Land, Politics and Nationalism: A Study of the Irish Land Question* (Dublin: Gill & Macmillan, 1996), p. 11.

95. Anthony Trollope, *The Landleaguers* [1883] (Oxford: Oxford University Press, 1993), p. 327.

96. Ibid., p. 346.

97. See L.P. Curtis Jnr, *Coercion and Conciliation, 1880–1892: A Study in Conservative Unionism* (Princeton: Princeton University Press, 1963), pp. 32–3.

98. Bull, *Land, Politics and Nationalism*, pp. 44–5.

99. *Hansard*, ser. 3, vol. 199, cols. 338–40, 386: a portmanteau quotation. Cited in Dewey, 'Celtic Agrarian Legislation', p. 59.

100. Indeed, the Crofters' Act of 1886, which was introduced by Gladstone in response to agitation among the crofting population of the Highlands and the islands, extended some of the provisions of the 1881 land Act to Scotland. These provisions included fixity of tenure and fair rent.

101. An editorial entitled 'Agrarian Bolshevism' published in the *Irish Times* on 29 April 1920 told of small farmers and landless peasants in the west who were forcing landholders, including the Congested Districts Board, to surrender property. The following month, landowners were advised by this unionist newspaper that the only way to put a stop to land seizures was to 'obtain some sort of control over the Sinn Féin movement'. 'Labour and the Land', *Irish Times*, 3 May 1920.

102. *Connacht Tribune*, 3 April 1920.

103. See David Fitzpatrick, 'Class, Family and Rural Unrest in Nineteenth-century Ireland', in P.J. Drudy (ed.), *Ireland: Land, Politics and People* (Cambridge: Cambridge University Press, 1982), pp. 37–75, p. 71.

104. Kevin O'Shiel, 'The Dáil Courts Driven Underground', *Irish Times*, 11 November 1966; 'The Dáil Land Courts', *Irish Times*,

14 November 1966; 'Years of Violence', *Irish Times*, 15 November 1966; 'Fellow Travellers', *Irish Times*, 17 November 1966; 'Dáil Courts in Action', *Irish Times*, 18 November 1966; 'No Contempt of Court', *Irish Times*, 21 November 1966; 'The Last Land War', *Irish Times*, 22 November 1966; 'On the Edge of Anarchy', *Irish Times*, 23 November 1966. See also Tony Varley, 'Agrarian Crime and Social Control: Sinn Féin and and the Land Question in the West of Ireland in 1920', in Ciaran McCullagh et al (eds), *Whose Law and Order? Aspects of Crime and Social Control in Irish Society* (Belfast: Sociological Association of Ireland, 1988), pp. 54–75, p. 58.

105. O'Shiel, 'The Last Land War', *Irish Times*, 22 November 1966.

106. Ó Tuathaigh, 'Irish Land Questions in the State of the Union', p. 11.

107. O'Shiel, 'No Contempt of Court', *Irish Times*, 21 November 1966.

108. O'Shiel, 'On the Edge of Anarchy', *Irish Times*, 23 November 1966.

109. Ibid.

110. Varley, 'Agrarian Crime and Social Control', p. 63.

111. See Gearóid Ó Tuathaigh, 'The Land Question, Politics and Irish Society, 1922–1960', in P.J. Drudy (ed.), *Ireland: Land, Politics and People* (Cambridge: Cambridge University Press, 1982), pp. 167–89, p. 169.

112. C. Desmond Greaves, *Liam Mellows and the Irish Revolution* [1917] (London: Lawrence and Wishart, 2004), pp. 114.

113. 'Welcome to the Decade of Centenaries Website', p. 1, http://www.decadeofcentenaries.com/ (accessed 30 November 2016).

114. Foster, *The Story of Ireland*, p. 27.

115. Kate Soper, 'Passing Glories and Romantic Retrievals: Avant-garde Nostalgia and Hedonist Renewal', in Axel Goodbody

and Kate Rigby (eds), *Ecocritical Theory: New European Approaches* (Charlottesville: University of Virginia Press, 2011), pp. 17–29, p. 24.

116. Ibid. In her theorisation of avant-garde nostalgia, Soper draws on the writings of the Marxist cultural theorist Raymond Williams. Indeed, the quotations included here are phrases that Soper cites from Williams' *Country and City* (1973). This section of her article also contains a brief discussion of Williams' 1983 book *Towards 2000*, in which he puts forward a strong critique of the modernising thrust.

117. Dobbins, *Whenever Green is Red*, p. 631.

118. Connolly, 'Erin's Hope', p. 8.

119. Dobbins, *Whenever Green is Red*, p. 629.

120. Ibid.

121. Cited in Martin, *Past Futures*, p. 192.

122. Charles Graves and James H. Todd, *Suggestions With a View to the Transcription and Publication of the Manuscripts of the Brehon Laws, Now in the Libraries of the British Museum, the University of Oxford, the Royal Irish Academy, and Trinity College, Dublin* (London: Macintosh Printer, 1851), p. 3.

123. W. Neilson Hancock and Thaddeus O'Mahony, 'Preface', *The Ancient Laws and Institutes of Ireland*, vol. II (London: Longman's, Green, Reader and Dyer, 1869), pp. v–lx, p. lvii.

124. It should be noted that the Brehon laws also legislated for the relationship – whether permanent, semi-permanent or transitory – between sexual partners who were not married. See ibid., p. lvi.

125. Mary Kotsonouris, *Retreat from Revolution: The Dáil Courts, 1920–24* (Dublin: Irish Academic Press, 1994), p. 5.

126. Cited in Henry Hanna, *The Statute Law of the Irish Free State (Saorstát Éireann), 1922 to 1928* (Dublin: A. Thom, 1929), pp. 30–1.

127. James Creed Meredith, 'Desirable Ameliorations of the Law', *Journal of the Statistical and Social Inquiry Society of Ireland*, vol. 16 (1939–40), pp. 63–74, p. 69.

128. Dorothy Macardle, *The Irish Republic* [1937] (Dublin: Irish Press Ltd, 1951), p. 346.

129. See ibid.

130. David Foxton, *Revolutionary Lawyers: Sinn Féin and Crown Courts in Ireland and Britain, 1916–1923* (Dublin: Four Courts Press, 2008), pp. 190–1. Incidentally, women could be Brehons in Gaelic Ireland. See Alice Stopford Green, *History of the Irish State to 1014* (London: Macmillan & Co, 1925), p. 205.

131. Sophie Bryant, *Liberty, Order and Law Under Native Irish Rule: A Study in the Book of the Ancient Laws of Ireland* (London: Harding & More, 1923), p. v.

132. Ibid., p. vii.

133. Ibid., p. viii.

134. Ibid., p. 88–9.

135. Bryant, an experienced mountaineer, died aged seventy-two while on a climbing holiday in Chamonix, France. The full circumstances of her death are unknown.

136. Benjamin, 'On the Concept of History', p. 391.

137. Ibid.

138. Ibid., p. 392.

139. Saint-Amour, *Tense Future*, p. 22.

140. Benjamin, 'On the Concept of History', p. 390.

141. Saint-Amour, *Tense Future*, p. 23.

142. Paul Ricoeur, *Amour et Justice* (Tübingen: J.C.B. Nohr, 1990), p. 58, cited in ibid., p. 245.

143. See, for example, Roy Foster's somewhat tongue-in-cheek account of the activities of the writer and activist Rosamond

Jacob: 'On a brief jaunt to Dublin ... in January 1911, the 23-year-old nationalist Rosamond Jacob first made her way to her Quaker relations ... where she met the radical-artistic *bon ton*, including the painter Sarah Purser and the academic Charles Oldham. Later she set off with Elizabeth Somers to the Inghinidhe rooms – six flights up, piles of the radical feminist journal *Bean na hÉireann* on the floor, pin-ups of Maud Gonne and 'John Brennan' (the journalist Sydney Gifford) on the walls, the latter in narrow skirts and smoking a cigarette. Jacob went on to inspect Hugh Lane's new gallery for modern art in Harcourt Street, and dined at the vegetarian restaurant in Westland Row ... Later she met her friend Edith White, a schools inspector and Gaelic enthusiast, at the Café Cairo in Grafton Street, and ordered some cream hopsack material at Kellett's drapery store to make herself a "national costume". Evening entertainments included a *soirée* at the Vegetarian Society, with harp music, and a Gaelic League *céilidh*'. Foster, *Vivid Faces*, pp. 8–9.

144. This tokenism was particularly evident in the incorporation of some black dancers and a large photograph of the unionist politician Edward Carson in the strange pseudo-Celtic dancing extravaganza that comprised the principal GAA 1916 commemoration in Croke Park on 24 April 2016.

145. Patrick Logue, 'Trump Dublin: US President Buys Liberty Hall to Build 5-Star Hotel', *Irish Times*, 1 April 2017.

146. Wills, *Dublin 1916*, p. 217.

147. This assertion is common to left-leaning assessments of the Rising. Thus, the opening article of *Jacobin*'s issue on the 1916 insurrection is titled 'Ireland's Unfinished Revolution'. Ronan Burtenshaw and Seán Byers, 'Ireland's Unfinished Revolution', *Jacobin*, no. 21 (spring 2016), pp. 11–20.

148. 'Rising Ideals Still Not Achieved, Says Higgins', *Irish Times* 30 March 2016.

149. 'Reclaim 1916: Reclaim the Vision of 1916', http://www.reclaim1916.ie/ (accessed 18 April 2017).

150. Connolly, 'Erin's Hope', pp. 3–4.

151. Robert Ballagh 'Speeches', p. 5, http://www.reclaim1916.ie/speeches/ (accessed 18 April 2017).

152. In *I Am Traveller*, Connors points out that when other actors involved in *Love/Hate* are interviewed, they were mostly asked such innocuous questions as whether they would like to work in Hollywood or who they would invite to their ideal dinner party. In contrast, he is invariably asked to comment on bare-knuckle boxing or the well-publicised feuds between certain Traveller families.

153. Trollope, *The Landleaguers*, pp. 346.

154. This same Ireland has built an entire tourism industry around Joyce's *Ulysses*, a novel in which Leopold Bloom is famously disparaged for his supposed lack of roots.

155. The ten people who died in the fire were Willy Lynch, Tara Gilbert and their daughters Kelsey and Jodie; Thomas and Sylvia Connors and three of their children Jimmy, Christy and Mary; and Jimmy Lynch, a brother of Willy Lynch and Sylvia Connors.

156. It is worth noting that literary critics have formed compelling connections between such narratives of personal development – as found in coming-of-age tales, particularly when concerned with young men – and progressivist models of history. See, for example, Jed Esty, *Unseasonable Youth: Modernism, Colonialism and the Fiction of Development* (Oxford: Oxford University Press, 2013).

157. Seamus Deane, 'Land and Soil: A Territorial Rhetoric', *History Ireland*, vol. 2, no. 1 (1994), pp. 31–4, p. 34.

158. Cited in McCabe, 'Sins of the Father', p. 57.

159. Ibid., p. 20. Owner-occupancy, it was argued, would free up rented accommodation and 'these vacancies would eventually filter down to the slums, allowing those who could afford the rents to move up the housing chain' (ibid., p. 16).

160. Ibid., p. 13.

161. Ibid.

162. See ibid., p. 57.

163. *The Travellers*, episode 3 (dir. Liam McGrath, Scratch Films). An alternative theory regarding the origins of Irish Travellers is put forward in this documentary. This theory, which draws on the DNA evidence gathered for the programme, suggests that the community split between the Traveller Irish and the settled Irish occured at a much earlier stage in Irish history, possibly during the early modern period when colonial authorities were seeking to displace a more communal system of succession and landholding with a form of absolute ownership more compatible with English property law. The ancestors of modern-day Travellers, according to this theory, were not settled people who lost their homes during the Famine, but those who resisted the introduction of a land system that would eventually create the kinds of conditions that contributed to the Famine.

164. 'Fianna Fáil did well because its leader Micheál Martin discerned what was happening and moved his party, rhetorically at least, onto mildly social democratic ground, promising greater fairness and investment in public services.' Fintan O'Toole, 'The Winner of Election 2016 is Social Democracy', *Irish Times*, 29 February 2016.

165. Editors' note: This theme is also addressed in the text on freedom in the Síreacht series where Two Fuse explore the idea of freedom as a rewriting or tearing up of (pre-)scripted practices of freedom that foreclose alternative ways of thinking and being. See Two Fuse, *Freedom?* (Cork: Cork University Press, 2017).

166. The recent Brexit vote in Britain, it has to acknowledged, also points to a multifarious future, though some of the roads that this vote points to are a cause of concern for anyone seeking a more just and equal world. This referendum, similar to the 2016 American elections, reveals the extent to which the public's hostility to neoliberalism can be used opportunistically to garner support for right-wing nationalism.

167. Dominic Byran, Mike Cronin, Tina O'Toole and Catriona Pennell, 'Ireland's Decade of Commemorations: A Roundtable', *New Hibernia Review*, vol. 17, no. 3 (2013), pp. 63–86, p. 82.

168. Catherine Chaput, *Inside the Teaching Machine: Rhetoric and the Globalisation of the U.S. Public Research University* (Tuscaloosa: University of Alabama Press, 2008), p. 245. Chaput distinguishes genuine transdisciplinary praxis from the interdisciplinary approaches advocated by university and professional organisations. According to Chaput, interdisciplinarity simultaneously challenges and reinforces the boundaries between disciplines in that it involves the collaboration of multiple, though separate, disciplines (p. 244).

169. Ibid., p. 245.

170. Ó Tuathaigh, 'Irish Land Questions in the State of the Union', p. 17.

171. Ibid.

172. 'Pitched Battle on Roadside', *Munster Express*, 29 November 1919.

173. Conor Kostick, 'Labour Militancy During the Irish War of Independence', in Fintan Lane and Donal Ó Drisceoil (eds), *Politics and the Irish Working Class, 1830–1945* (Basingstoke: Palgrave Macmillan, 2005), pp. 187–206, p. 189. See also Emmet O'Connor, 'Agrarian Unrest and the Labour Movement in Co. Waterford, 1917–1923 ', *Saothar: Journal of Irish Labour History*, vol. 6 (1980), pp. 40–58, p. 41.

174. Fergus Campbell, *Land and Revolution: Nationalist Politics in the West of Ireland, 1891–1921* (Oxford: Oxford University Press, 2005), p. 280. In relation to the Creggs Land Committee, see also Kevin O'Shiel, 'The Dáil Land Courts', *Irish Times*, 14 November 1966.

175. Kostick, 'Labour Militancy', p. 188.

176. Campbell, *Land and Revolution*, p. 280.

177. Fergus Campbell, '*Land and Revolution* Revisited', in Fergus Campbell and Tony Varley (eds), *Land Questions in Modern Ireland* (Manchester: Manchester University Press, 2013), pp. 149–72, p. 152.

178. 'Initial Statement by Advisory Group on Centenary Commemorations', p. 5, http://www.decadeofcentenaries. com/initial-statement-by-advisory-group-on-centenary-commemorations/ (accessed 30 November 2016).

179. When conducting research on popular unrest for his seminal publication *Elementary Aspects of Peasant Insurgency in Colonial India* (Delhi: Oxford University Press, 1983), Ranajit Guha, the founding member of the Subaltern Studies Collective, became increasingly aware of the biased nature of official records, including police reports and administrative accounts, leading him to assert that 'evidence of this type has a way of stamping the interests and outlook of the rebels' enemies on every account of our peasant rebellions' (Guha, *Elementary Aspect*, p. 14).

180. Paul Cullen, 'Apollo House Activists to Meet Owners', *Irish Times*, 19 December 2016.

181. As Una Mullally points out, 'that's nearly seven times the size of St Stephen's Green park'. Una Mullally, 'Home Sweet Home is the Real "New Politics"', *Irish Times*, 19 December 2016.

182. Frederic Jameson, 'Future City', *New Left Review*, vol. 21 (2003) pp. 65–79, p. 76.

183. Enzo Traverso, *Marxism, History, and Memory* (New York: Columbia University Press, 2016), pp. 117–18.

Bibliography

Benjamin, Walter, 'On the Concept of History', in Howard Eiland and Michael W. Jennings (eds), *Walter Benjamin: Selected Writings*, vol. 4 (Cambridge MA: Belknap Press of Harvard University Press, 2006)

Bernstein, Michael André, *Foregone Conclusions: Against Apocalyptic History* (Berkeley: University of California Press, 1994)

Byran, Dominic, Mike Cronin, Tina O'Toole and Catriona Pennell, 'Ireland's Decade of Commemorations: A Roundtable', *New Hibernia Review*, vol. 17, no. 3 (2013)

Bryant, Sophie, *Liberty, Order and Law Under Native Irish Rule: A Study in the Book of the Ancient Laws of Ireland* (London: Harding & More, 1923)

Bull, Philip, *Land, Politics and Nationalism: A Study of the Irish Land Question* (Dublin: Gill & Macmillan, 1996)

Burtenshaw, Ronan and Seán Byers, 'Ireland's Unfinished Revolution', *Jacobin*, no. 21 (2016)

Campbell, Fergus, *Land and Revolution: Nationalist Politics in the West of Ireland, 1891–1921* (Oxford: Oxford University Press, 2005)

Campbell, Fergus and Tony Varley, *Land Questions in Modern Ireland* (Manchester: Manchester University Press, 2013)

Chaput, Catherine, *Inside the Teaching Machine: Rhetoric and the Globalisation of the U.S. Public Research University* (Tuscaloosa: University of Alabama Press, 2008)

Connerton, Paul, *How Societies Remember* (Cambridge: Cambridge University Press, 1989)

Connolly, James, 'Erin's Hope: The End and the Means' [1897], in Donal Nevin (ed.), *Writings of James Connolly*, vol. 2 (Dublin: SIPTU, 2011)

Curtis Jnr, L.P., *Coercion and Conciliation in Ireland, 1880–1892: A Study in Conservative Unionism* (Princeton: Princeton University Press, 1963)

Daly, Mary E. and Margaret O'Callaghan (eds), *1916 in 1966: Commemorating the Easter Rising* (Dublin: Royal Irish Academy, 2007)

Davitt, Michael, *The Fall of Feudalism in Ireland, or the Story of the Land League Revolution* (London: Harper & Brothers, 1904)

Deane, Seamus, 'Land and Soil: A Territorial Rhetoric', *History Ireland*, vol. 2, no. 1 (1994)

Dewey, Clive, 'Celtic Agrarian Legislation and the Celtic Revival: Historicist Implications of Gladstone's Irish and Scottish Land Acts 1870–1886', *Past & Present*, no. 64 (1974)

Dobbins, Gregory, 'Connolly, the Archive, and Method', *Interventions: International Journal of Postcolonial Studies*, vol. 10, no. 1 (2008)

————. 'Whenever Green is Red: James Connolly and Postcolonial Theory', *Nepantla: Views from the South*, vol. 1, no. 3 (2000)

Drudy, P.J. (ed.), *Ireland: Land, Politics and People* (Cambridge: Cambridge University Press, 1982)

Elices, John F., 'Uchronian Scenarios in the Context of Irish Literature: The Case of C.B. Gilford's *The Crooked Shamrock*', *Estudios Irelandeses*, no. 9 (2014)

Esty, Jed, *Unseasonable Youth: Modernism, Colonialism and the Fiction of Development* (Oxford: Oxford University Press, 2013)

Fitzpatrick, David, 'The Disappearance of the Irish Agricultural Labourer, 1841–1912', *Irish Economic and Social History*, vol. 7 (1980)

Foster, Roy, *The Story of Ireland* (Oxford: Oxford University Press, 1995)

———. *Vivid Faces: The Revolutionary Generation in Ireland, 1890–1923* (London: Allen Lane, 2014)

Foxton, David, *Revolutionary Lawyers: Sinn Féin and Crown Courts in Ireland and Britain, 1916–1923* (Dublin: Four Courts Press, 2008)

Goodbody, Axel and Kate Rigby (eds), *Ecocritical Theory: New European Approaches* (Charlottesville: University of Virginia Press, 2011)

Graves, Charles and James H. Todd, *Suggestions With a View to the Transcription and Publication of the Manuscripts of the Brehon Laws, Now in the Libraries of the British Museum, the University of Oxford, the Royal Irish Academy, and Trinity College, Dublin* (London: Macintosh Printer, 1851)

Greaves, C. Desmond, *Liam Mellows and the Irish Revolution* [1971] (London: Lawrence and Wishart, 2004)

Green, Alice Stopford, *History of the Irish State to 1014* (London: Macmillan & Co, 1925)

Guha, Ranajit, *Elementary Aspects of Peasant Insurgency in Colonial India* (Delhi: Oxford University Press, 1983)

Hancock, Neilson W. and Thaddeus O'Mahony (eds), *The Ancient Laws and Institutes of Ireland*, vol. ii (London: Longman's, Green, Reader and Dyer, 1869)

Hanna, Henry, *The Statute Law of the Irish Free State (Saorstát Éireann), 1922 to 1928* (Dublin: A. Thom, 1929)

Higgins, Róisín, *Transforming 1916: Meaning, Memory and the Fiftieth Anniversary of the Easter Rising* (Cork: Cork University Press, 2012)

Hobsbawm, Eric, *Primitive Rebels: Studies in Archaic Forms of Social Movement in the Nineteenth and Twentieth Centuries* (Manchester: Manchester University Press, 1959)

Horne, John and Edward Madigan (eds), *Towards Commemoration: Ireland in War and Revolution, 1912–23* (Dublin: Royal Irish Academy, 2013)

Iggers, Georg G. and James M. Powell (eds), *Leopold von Ranke and the Shaping of the Historical Discipline* (Syracuse: Syracuse University Press, 1990)

Jameson, Frederic, 'Future City', *New Left Review*, vol. 21 (2003)

Joyce, James, *Dubliners* [1914] (Harmondsworth: Penguin, 1992)

———. *Ulysses* [1922] (Harmondsworth: Penguin, 1972)

Kelleher, Margaret and James H. Murphy (eds), *Gender Perspectives in Nineteenth Century Ireland: Public and Private Spheres* (Dublin: Irish Academic Press, 1997)

Kostick, Conor, *Revolution in Ireland: Popular Militancy, 1917–23* (London: Pluto Press, 1996)

Koselleck, Reinhart, *Futures Past: On the Semantics of Historical Time* (Cambridge, MA: MIT Press, 1985)

Kotsonouris, Mary, *Retreat from Revolution: The Dáil Courts, 1920–24* (Dublin: Irish Academic Press, 1994)

Krieger, Leonard, *Ranke: The Meaning of History* (Chicago: University of Chicago Press, 1977)

Laird, Heather, *Subversive Law in Ireland: From 'Unwritten Law' to the Dáil Courts* (Dublin: Four Courts Press, 2005)

Lane, Fintan and Donal Ó Drisceoil (eds), *Politics and the Irish Working Class, 1830–1945* (Basingstoke: Palgrave Macmillan, 2005)

Lerner, Gerda, *The Majority Finds its Past: Placing Women in History* (Oxford: Oxford University Press, 1979)

Lloyd, David, 'Rethinking National Marxism: James Connolly and "Celtic Communism"', *Interventions: International Journal of Postcolonial Studies*, vol. 5, no. 3 (2003)

————. 'The Subaltern in Motion: Subalternity, the Popular and Irish Working Class History', *Postcolonial Studies*, vol. 8, no. 4 (2006)

Macardle, Dorothy, *The Irish Republic* [1937] (Dublin: Irish Press Ltd., 1951)

Martin, Ged, *Past Futures: The Impossible Necessity of History* (Toronto: Toronto University Press, 2004)

McBride, Ian (ed.), *History and Memory in Modern Ireland* (Cambridge: Cambridge University Press, 2001)

McCabe, Conor, *Sins of the Father: The Decisions that Shaped the Irish Economy*, revised edn (Dublin: The History Press Ireland, 2013)

McCarthy, Conor, *Modernisation: Crisis and Culture in Ireland, 1969–1992* (Dublin: Four Courts Press, 2000)

————. *The Revolutionary and Anti-imperial Writings of James Connolly, 1893–1916* (Edinburgh: Edinburgh University Press, 1916)

MacGill, Patrick, *Children of the Dead End* (London: Herbert Jenkins, 1914)

————. *The Rat Pit* (London: Herbert Jenkins, 1915)

Meredith, James Creed, 'Desirable Ameliorations of the Law', *Journal of the Statistical and Social Inquiry Society of Ireland*, vol. 16 (1939–40)

Mill, John Stuart, *England and Ireland* (London: Longmans, Green, Reader and Dyer, 1868)

O'Connor, Emmet, 'Agrarian Unrest and the Labour Movement in Co. Waterford, 1917–1923', *Saothar: Journal of Irish Labour History*, vol. 6 (1980)

O'Donnell, Peadar, *Adrigoole* (London: Jonathan Cape, 1929)

O'Sullivan, Donal J., *The Irish Constabularies, 1822–1922: A Century of Policing in Ireland* (Dingle, Co. Kerry: Brandon, 1999)

Reid, Colin, *The Lost Ireland of Stephen Gwynn: Irish Constitutional Nationalism and Cultural Politics 1864–1950* (Manchester: Manchester University Press, 2011)

Saint-Amour, Paul K., *Tense Future: Modernisation, Total War, Encyclopedic Form* (Oxford: Oxford University Press, 2015)

Scott, David, *Conscripts of Modernity: The Tragedy of Colonial Enlightenment* (Durham: Duke University Press, 2004)

Shaw, George Bernard, *Back to Methuselah: A Metabiological Pentateuch* [1921] (Harmondsworth: Penguin, 1977)

———. *John Bull's Other Island* [1904] (Harmondsworth: Penguin, 1984)

Thompson, E.P., *The Making of the English Working Class* (London: Victor Gollancz, 1963)

Traverso, Enzo, *Left-wing Melancholia: Marxism, History, and Memory* (New York: Columbia University Press, 2016)

Trollope, Anthony, *The Landleaguers* [1883] (Oxford: Oxford University Press, 1993)

Varley, Tony, 'Agrarian Crime and Social Control: Sinn Féin and the Land Question in the West of Ireland in 1920', in Ciarán McCullagh et al (eds), *Whose Law and Order?: Aspects of Crime and Social Control in Irish Society* (Belfast: Sociological Association of Ireland, 1988)

Wills, Clair, *Dublin 1916: The Siege of the GPO* (London: Profile Books, 2009)

Winter, Jay, *Sites of Memory, Sites of Mourning: The Great War in European Cultural History* (Cambridge: Cambridge University Press, 1998)

Yeates, Pádraig (ed.), *The Workers' Republic: James Connolly and the Road to the Rising* (Dublin: SIPTU, 2015)

Yeats, W.B., *Selected Poems* (London: Phoenix, 2002)

Index

Note: illustrations are indicated by page numbers in bold.